RESPECTING ANIMALS

RESPECTING ANIMALS

ANIMALS

A **BALANCED APPROACH**
to Our Relationship with
PETS, **FOOD**, and **WILDLIFE**

DAVID S. FAVRE

Prometheus Books
59 John Glenn Drive
Amherst, New York 14228

Published 2018 by Prometheus Books

Respecting Animals: A Balanced Approach to Our Relationship with Pets, Food, and Wildlife.
Copyright © 2018 by David S. Favre. All rights reserved. No part of this publication may be reproduced, stored in a retrieval system, or transmitted in any form or by any means, digital, electronic,
mechanical, photocopying, recording, or otherwise, or conveyed via the internet or a website
without prior written permission of the publisher, except in the case of brief quotations embodied
in critical articles and reviews.

Trademarked names appear throughout this book. Prometheus Books recognizes all registered
trademarks, trademarks, and service marks mentioned in the text.

Cover images © Shutterstock
Cover design by Nicole Sommer-Lecht
Cover design © Prometheus Books

The internet addresses listed in the text were accurate at the time of publication. The inclusion
of a website does not indicate an endorsement by the author(s) or by Prometheus Books, and
Prometheus Books does not guarantee the accuracy of the information presented at these sites.

Inquiries should be addressed to
Prometheus Books
59 John Glenn Drive
Amherst, New York 14228
VOICE: 716–691–0133 • FAX: 716–691–0137
WWW.PROMETHEUSBOOKS.COM

22 21 20 19 18   5 4 3 2 1

Library of Congress Cataloging-in-Publication Data Pending

Printed in the United States of America

Dedicated to my forever wife, Marty Favre,
having traveled the road of life together.

CONTENTS

CONTENTS

CHAPTER 9. PAUSE AND REFOCUS 115

CHAPTER 10. THE PROCESS OF MAKING JUDGMENTS 119

CHAPTER 11. VALUES 139

CHAPTER 12. ETHICAL JUDGMENTS ABOUT ANIMALS 149

CONTENTS

CONTENTS

FOREWORD

BY BERNARD E. ROLLIN,

AUTHOR OF *A NEW BASIS FOR ANIMAL ETHICS*

W hen I published my first book on animal ethics in 1981, *Animal Rights and Human Morality*, it had become clear to me that it was essential to move the law toward taking greater account of animal interests. During the ensuing years, it has become increasingly evident to society in general that the law is a powerful tool for raising the status of animals. Thus, for example, in 2004, there were 2,100 pieces of legislation floated in federal, state, and local legislatures in the United States aimed at enhancing the welfare of animals.[1] The societal thrust has continued to grow. In 2003, a Gallup poll indicated that approximately 70 percent of the US public wish to see legislated constraints on how farm animals could be raised. When the survey was recently repeated in 2012, the number had risen to 94 percent. This point is further buttressed by referenda aimed at limiting the most egregious confinement of farm animals—veal crates, sow stalls, and battery cages for chickens. In each state that the referendum was floated, it passed by a 2 to 1 margin.

Professor Favre was a key player—along with a number of other lawyers in the early 1980s, most notably Joyce Tischler—in creating Attorneys for Animal Rights, later known as the Animal Legal Defense Fund. Thanks to these attorneys, most law schools now have courses in animal law, and there are many animal lawyers. My own legal work in the mid-1980s successfully aimed at legislatively rectifying the failure of the research community to utilize analgesia for painful animal protocols, and at goading veterinary medicine into teaching analgesia and modeling its use, with the legislation passing through Congress in 1985. In effect, what was created was a legal right for animals utilized in painful research to have their pain controlled. By being enshrined in federal law, pain control ipso facto became the standard of care in veterinary medicine.

The present book powerfully evidences that Favre has a mind unlikely to get caught in a rut. As he indicates, he soon came to realize that the total abolitionist point of view of animal ethics was not likely to be a very effective engine of change, and that meaningful change advancing the interests of animals was morally essential. This book chronicles, in a lyrical and persuasive way, his intellectual and personal odyssey toward this goal. In particular, he recounts moving from the suburbs onto a very traditional, husbandry-based sheep farm, and the lessons he learned from that transition, as well as the rich understanding of animal life and nature that transition entailed.

Utilizing a variety of rhetorical methods, ranging from rational argument, to poetry, to photographs, to personal anecdote, Favre advances an approach to animal welfare that he accurately describes as "respectful use." Respectful use, as he explains, cannot be effected by simple algorithms. There is a strong element of intuition derived from emotional responses and reflection thereon involved in recognizing respectful use. Thus he argues that corporate industrialized animal agriculture does not instantiate respectful use, whereas small family farms rooted in the ancient concept of good husbandry that initially made animal agriculture possible, and in sustainable use of resources, if properly run, do. Similarly, hunting for food in a manner aimed at minimizing animal distress and suffering also does, whereas trophy hunting does not. Perceptively, he acknowledges that identifying respectful use requires an admixture of reason and intuition, head and heart.

As Favre readily acknowledges, recognizing the basic needs and interests of animals "as determined by their DNA," is an essential component of using them respectfully. In my own work, I express this notion by reference to the essential nature of an animal, what Aristotle calls *Telos*. As

I have indicated elsewhere, expressing *Telos* can be more important to animals even than pain and distress.

Another significant difference between Favre and most other animal ethicists is that he focuses not only on individual animals but also on species in their ecological context. He has great respect for ecological science and uses the knowledge therefrom in advancing his arguments.

This is not a book providing pat answers to the difficult questions that arise when one begins to contemplate our moral obligations to other creatures. Indeed, Favre himself stimulates the readers' thoughts with many difficult questions. For example, how does one balance the interests of the animals confined in a zoo with the pleasures that zoos bring to those who visit them? How does one balance feeding a predatory animal in confinement live prey, as dictated by its nature, against the suffering of the prey animal? What this book does is help the reader focus his or her thinking on these issues in a new way, ideally creating a gestalt shift in how these issues are viewed.

Having devoted more than forty years to wrestling with animal ethics and attempting to effect change in numerous areas of animal use, I greatly appreciate and value the perspective that Favre is attempting to instill in readers of this book, and I know that I will continue to benefit from it in my own activities.

ACKNOWLEDGMENTS

The drafting of this book took many years and the support of a number of individuals. Michigan State University College of Law (previously known as the Detroit College of Law), has always supported my efforts on behalf of animals, even at the beginning point back in the 1980s. Without that support, my intellectual path forward would have been almost impossible.

A number of people have reviewed various drafts of this book and provided useful suggestions, questions, and comments: Brittany Mouzourakis, Karen Chopra, Jeremy Francis, Charles Roboski, Tom Wright, Kimberli A. Bindschatel, and Yoshida Akimune—and, of course, my editor at Prometheus Books, Steven L. Mitchell. I am most appreciative of the efforts of my son, Scott Favre, and his wife, Jennifer Haeger, in the reviewing my materials.

"Humans do not easily surround themselves with truth. It is an elusive beast to find and hold fast. But is it a hunt that must be undertaken."

—David S. Favre, 2012

INTRODUCTION

Admittedly the title *Respecting Animals* might be a bit ambitious, but after having spent a lifetime peeling back the layers of the animal/human issues, at the core I found some simple but significant concepts that can be used to guide human decision-making about animals. The nature of the problem is that as I peeled back the onion, the concepts became rather sweeping in scope, but that is not my fault. It is clear when you get to the center of a real onion, there is no place else to go; but if you peel an idea-onion, the center can be an elusive space. It is impossible to know when there is only one more idea. Now my thoughts try to encompass all of life (at least all of life that is visible to me). I will not seek any more layers of the onion. With this book, I seek to describe what I have found as best I can.

Humans are enmeshed in a web of life that for most of us contains both wildlife and domestic animals. Millions of pets, companion animals, have a positive life. Unfortunately, for billions of commercial domestic animals, it is not a positive life. While the welfare and suffering of pets are clearly issues before us, as they are physically before us, the death and suffering of wildlife is neither seen nor contemplated by most humans. More and more wildlife are dying as a consequence of the human plague scouring across Earth.

We need a reset, a reconsideration of the relationship between human beings and the other living beings of this planet. Anyone viewing Earth from high above in time-lapse pictures would perceive that humans are seeking to kill the wildlife of the planet by either consuming them as food (e.g., tuna and sharks), destroying their living places (e.g., the growth of palm oil plantations), or transforming them into products for commercial consumption (e.g., elephants and ivory). It is not a pretty picture. Some of the significant factors that got us to this place include too many humans, capitalism running amok, unseen billions of animals killed every year (e.g., chickens and fish), and human ignorance of their impact on other beings that share this earth. This is a good planet; it is our only planet. Should we care about all of these other beings? Is there a path forward for the human individuals in our society who do care about these other beings?

A path forward does exist, and it has a signpost. Written upon the signpost is: Respectful Use. The destination is an indeterminable distance and time away, but it is a place and time where humans will use animals only in the context of respectful use. While it is a simple phrase, it provides a powerful limitation on action when interwoven into the minds of human beings. The idea of respect has a logical, rational component, but it also has an emotional, holist one with roots in human judgments about fairness and justice. This book shall consider why we should think about animals, how we got where we are, and how to walk down the path of respectful use.

Something that this book does not do is consider the realm of religion and whether it plays a role in how humans got to this point of planetary risk or whether religion can play a role in moving us forward. My simple answer is that even though religion is a powerful force in the lives of millions, even billions, of humans, it may or may not be helpful for where we are today or for our future on this planet. Western religions are personal with a focus on living an appropriate life in the eyes of their god and a primary concern about what will happen after the death of the individual. While many religious-based voices have spoken up about the environment and animal issues, it seems to have had only a modest effect. I am without sufficient information to understand Eastern religions. Notwithstanding centuries of religious teaching, countries of the East have significant human overpopulation issues as well as levels of pollution and resource consumption that are not good for humans or animals. Their legal systems barely touch upon the welfare of animals. Therefore, even though a call to respectful use of living beings will hopefully have a positive resonance in many of the religions of the world, those paths will not be considered in these pages. Perhaps others might take up such a task.

The question of animal/human relationships will be contemplated at two levels. The first is in an individual ethical context of how to lead an individual life. The second is a social context in which the law comes into play. No individual human has total freedom to act on personal judgment; the social rules of ethics step in to prevent it. Adoption of law is an outcome of social judgment. Thus, humans are in theory constrained by law to not murder other human beings, even if a particular human, after thoughtful consideration, believes it is acceptable and necessary to murder another human. The restraints of law allow us the freedom to live our daily lives by acknowledging the presence and legal rights of others. The concept of respectful use will need to be transferred into the legal system, since many humans seem incapable of respecting animals. However, development of personal ethics usually precedes adoption of legal standards.

The ethics of philosophy[1] or religion seek to organize our thoughts and help us structure our daily activities within a worldview with which we are comfortable. Within this book the focus is upon animals. Most Americans interact daily with animals, be it the food we eat, the cat we pet, the bird we observe in a tree, or the entertainment we enjoy. How do we think about these animals? How ought we to think about these animals? Ethics presumes we have choices in our lives, and an ethical framework seeks to help us make those choices. Usually, choices turn into habits, which are repetitive actions that do not require thinking about the appropriateness of the action. But often the actions of an individual are based not upon ethical considerations, but upon community or family culture, which is a set of unexamined but acted-upon premises.

The tail of the dog is docked or the cat declawed because others do it, or your family did it in the past. You go hunting or to the zoo because you did so as a child, and may well have positive memories surrounding such events. Individuals seldom have deep conversations with themselves about these habit-based activities unless a trigger event occurs. Something arises to bring into question why you are doing or are about to do something. Others may raise a question that you cannot get out of your head, or an event might occur that causes self-reflection. Perhaps a law is passed that causes difficulties or prohibits what you did in the past.

Consider your family trip to the local zoo. It's a nice day; the family is together; and the environment is pleasant. You pass by the exhibits, a chimpanzee in one, a group of flamingos in another, or perhaps a building with snakes of all sizes that young children find greatly interesting. Perhaps you spend more than thirty seconds before the chimpanzee and actually look at the animal. You see sadness, stress, a limp, and an otherwise-empty cage. It might be enough to trigger internal questions: "What is this animal doing here? Is this good for the animal?" Will that seed of thought take root and result in a contemplation of the issue of whether it is acceptable to use wild animals as zoo exhibits so that human families can have a pleasant afternoon? Maybe, maybe not.

For the average person, the issue may arise as a less formal question, but still a powerful one: "Should that chimpanzee (bird or snake) be in that cage?" In the more formal world of ethics, the presence of animals in a zoo gives rise to formal statements of the issue, such as "Are the limitations of life and well-being for animals in a zoo ethically justified by humans experiencing pleasant days of entertainment?" When an individual sees an animal at the zoo as more than just passing eye candy ("Oh, Mom, look at that!"), then the possibility of internal or family discussions may arise. When people see the animal, be it a chimpanzee or squirrel monkey, they might think, "This is a being, it has had a life before I passed by and will continue with its life after I pass by. What kind of life is it? Is the animal well taken care of; will it have a natural life? Is this good for the animal? Does it make any difference to me if it is not a good life for the animal?"

Perhaps your family decides to take a trip out into the country to visit the great places where your parents used to camp when they were children. With stories of streams flowing over rocks, deer and bears in the woods, and ducks and cranes on the lake, you cross the crest of the hill and find that suburbia has arrived. While the two-hundred-acre state park is still there, the surrounding landscape has been transformed. There is no room for bear or deer. The stream survives among construction debris, and the lake is barren and lifeless. You reflect: "What has happened to the land, to the wildlife?" Although these animals were also entertainment for the human visitors, unlike the zoo, this is a place that was the natural home for the wildlife. Perhaps you will have another conversation with yourself: "Is it a good thing that human development has supplanted the home of the wildlife? Is it fair that human activity has driven out the prior diversity of life?"

What concepts and principles will be useful in seeking the answers to these questions? Perhaps you ask, "Is the keeping of the animals lawful?" This is not the best first question. The discussion of animal/human relationships requires that the ethical/cultural context be considered first, then the role of the law can be considered. In the United States, we have a long legal history of concern for animal welfare, but that will be the starting point for my next book.[2]

Subsequent chapters will propose that a primary context for deciding what is an ethical outcome for animal/human interactions is the community in which both the human and animal exist. Do they coexist in a commercial farm world or in the home, companionship world? Perhaps the community is the relationship of humans with wild beings in the oceans of the world. While some argue that any animal, or any human, is due the same ethical treatment in all circumstances, I reject this simplistic approach both for humans and for animals. As my ethical duties toward my son or daughter are different from my ethical duty toward strangers around the world, so my ethical duty to my companion animal is different from that to an animal at the local zoo.

INTRODUCTION

Primarily, the task of this book is to propose a comprehensive vision of how animals can be significantly integrated into the lives of humans, not as full equals but as individuals and groups deserving respectful awareness by us—as individuals within the community with status to use legal rights to protect their most vital interests. As the four-year-old human child is not equal to an adult in rights or responsibilities, so the animal should not be considered equal to the child or the adult human in rights and responsibilities.

While the rabbit in the bush, the rabbit in the cage at a research center, and the rabbit in someone's living room may be biologically equivalent, they are not and cannot be considered identical in an ethical sense. It is the human context that is critical to the justifiable expectations for the rabbit. Biological similarities do not necessarily result in equal treatment under the law; it is more complex than that. Likewise, animal biological similarities to humans are not sufficient to build a house of ethics. The situation is more difficult.

This book will seek to provide some blending between two very distinct worldviews. The first has a focus on the welfare of individual animals. This view arises primarily out of the experience of humans having companion animals and knowing them as distinct individuals. The second view is about the nature and existence of ecosystems, which may contain a great diversity of animals that are unseen as individuals. The environmental perspective is about the existence and health of complex ecosystems. Most environmentalists do not focus on the welfare of individual animals within the various ecosystems. Those who focus their intellectual energy solely on the individual animals, particularly the beloved pet, must understand the limited context in which such animals live and must not expect extrapolation of that status to other animals, particularly wildlife. The environmentalist and the animalist will need to move toward each other.

Although I have an ethical path to suggest for the reader, I do not pretend to have all the answers. Any teacher of ideas knows that the best learning arises when the teacher provides some information for context but then leads the student forward with questions that trigger self-reflection. A primary goal of this book is to provide the reader with a comprehensive and useful context in which to consider personal and social relationships with animals. I am pleased that you are allowing me to lead you forward on this journey of self-discovery.

CHAPTER 1

AN ETHICAL DUTY TOWARD ANIMALS

We humans share Earth with millions of other species. We share ecosystems with these other species. We share a genetic history, shaped by evolution, with other beings. Is there any duty humans have toward individuals of all these other species? Or perhaps to the various species as sets of individuals? Are there any restraints on human actions or affirmative obligations toward these other beings? Perhaps these beings are conscious, perhaps not. Some feel pain, some do not. Some have a capacity to suffer, and others do not. Are they just physical things to use or not, as might be useful or entertaining to humans? If our diet requires protein, may we take it wherever it might be found? If we are entertained by death, may we inflict it? Do animals count for anything in our lives?

One restraint on human action is found under the umbrella of ethics (other umbrellas include law, religion, and family practices). Ethics are sets of ideas or social rules that shape human conduct. Ethics have as a starting point the presumption that in a particular set of circumstances a human has a choice of which conduct to pursue. And, by rational consideration, some conduct is considered preferable or more acceptable than other paths of conduct. For example, consider the following: a man, Homer, leaves his car, then he opens the front door of his home. It has been a hard, stressful day; the traffic has been terrible and he is hungry. Upon entering the door, he finds that his dog, Rover, is lying asleep on the floor. The options before him about what to do next are numerous:

Ignore the dog and step around it
Step on the dog
Kick the dog
Yell at the dog
Call the dog
Pet the dog
Hug the dog
Etc., etc.

How might we judge these options? What needs to be taken into account? What if it was a ball rather than a dog? What if it was his six-month-old son? Initially, there is the consideration of what impact the different actions would have upon Homer himself. Perhaps some actions would make him feel better. Some might have initial positive consequences, but later cause regret. Other actions would have no impact on Homer. The presence of an impact on Homer of a particular action does not make it an ethical question. Ethics has to do with relationships with others, the impact or consequences of one person's action or inaction on other persons. If a human child were on the floor, then the list of actions would presumably have some positive and some negative consequences to the child, thus making the possible actions by Homer an ethical question.

Whether an action is ethically positive or negative is determined by weighing the foreseeable consequences of the proposed action. To give a child a vaccine shot in the arm will have the immediate negative consequence of pain, but the subsequent benefits of health enhancement offset the initial negative. Therefore, the action is a positive ethical act. But most of us would judge that the risk of both short- and long-term harm and pain that would be the consequence of Homer stepping or kicking or even yelling at the child is not justified by the possible positive emotional release that might be felt by Homer. His kicking, stepping on, or yelling at the child would be judged by most to be unethical, a negative ethical action. One would hope that Homer's own judgment would come to the same conclusion and those actions would be rejected by him. If within a particular society there is strong majority opinion that agrees that certain specific actions are unacceptable, then a law can be passed prohibiting, for example, the kicking or stepping on a child, anyone's child. (Yelling at his child is much more difficult to judge both in ethics and in law.)

I would hope that everyone would agree that children of any age are "beings" included in the ethical universe of humans. In other words, they are "ethical subjects." We adult humans are "ethical actors" and have the obligation to consider the consequences of our actions upon ethical subjects. This obligation exists even if the ethical subject is not capable of accepting a reciprocal duty. For instance, the adult should not hit the child, but the restriction on the child to not hit the adult, to become an ethical actor, does not arise until the child is old enough to control his or her actions and have awareness of the consequences of those actions on ethical subjects. Initially, the human child, while being an ethical subject, might hit his sister without fully understanding the infliction of pain. At this point the child is not an ethical actor. But, as time passes and his brain develops, he will become an ethical actor, and restraint would be expected. He may hit his sister, specifically to inflict pain, and then the ethical teaching (or religious or family values) begins. He will be expected to conform to the ethical values (i.e., the preexisting judgments about acceptable and unacceptable conduct) within his community.

If Homer is faced with a ball on the floor, he may indeed realize a release of tension and stress if he kicks the ball very hard, a positive consequence of the action. While such a kick may have certain physical consequences within the house, are there ethical concerns about the consequences of the act to the ball itself? I think not. As an inanimate object, the ball cannot feel pain or suffer; the ball does not care about its own existence at any level. It is not alive. We may need to respect the ball because it is the property of another, but the ball is not "another" in and of itself. The ball is not an ethical subject.

We are left with the threshold question: What should Homer do or not do upon entering his house? Is Rover more like the ball or the baby? The dog is alive, as is the baby; the dog has preferences about life and the conduct of humans around him. The dog has a name; the ball does not. Our common experiences support a position that the dog would prefer a hug over a kick. So, would it be ethical for Homer to kick Rover? Common sense suggests the positive ethical choice for Homer is to not kick or step upon the dog. In saying this we necessarily admit the dog into our world of ethics. The dog is an ethical subject, a being whose interests must be taken into account when deciding to do something that impacts the being. Within the United States and many, if not most, countries of the world, it is presently accepted that it is wrong, unethical, to inflict unnecessary pain or suffering upon animals. Whether it is illegal is a separate question. Homer's bad day would not justify kicking, hitting, or stepping upon the dog since the negative consequences to the dog are not outweighed by the possible positive consequences to Homer. (A fair analysis might find that kicking the dog, regardless of immediate emotional release, is a negative for Homer's long-term well-being because it reinforces a socially negative state of aggression against others as an acceptable course of action.)

What if the animal was not our lovable dog but a turtle? It is safe to say the turtle is not as complex a being as a dog, but at some level a turtle feels pain and will withdraw from pain. Does a less-complex consciousness now allow the human benefit to outweigh that of the animal? No. But what if it was a ten-pound jellyfish? Do jellyfish experience pain? I don't know. Kicking a jellyfish seems like a stupid thing to do, but we will set that example in the gray area of ethics and refocus on the 89.7 million or so dogs that do exist in homes.[1]

If ethical analysis informs us about what Homer should not do, might it inform us about what he should do? Building again upon our common experiences of both humans and dogs, the optimum course of action should be that he hugs the dog. This will produce positive outcomes for Homer (a release of stress) and a positive outcome for the dog (the reinforcement of being an accepted member of Homer's family). As we proceed through the book, the difference between prohibiting the negative and requiring the positive will remain important. The full scope of duty can be discussed only after we establish what type of community the animal and the human share, which in this case is that of extended human family. I will have more to say about the concept of community later.

The above example uses the capacity for pain and suffering as the distinguishing feature of who might be an ethical subject. There is considerable debate among us ethical actors about where to draw the line between beings that are within and outside of our human ethical universe—about whom or what is an ethical subject. Indeed, Steve Wise, attorney and founder of the Nonhuman Rights Organization, has written a book on the topic titled *Drawing the Line*.[2] Other writers want to have a discussion about consciousness, with ethical duties arising only if a species can be shown to possess a particular level of consciousness. But there is little agreement about how to define consciousness, and indeed it may mean different things to different people. For the moment, it is important to agree that there are at least some animals, primarily mammals, that because of a number of species characteristics are clearly within our ethical universe. Since ethics are personal in nature, each person can decide for him- or herself if flies and oysters are within their ethical world. We can argue with each other endlessly because consensus is not required for individuals to act upon their own ethical precepts. Note that consensus on ethical precepts will be important in defining human communities and the laws adopted within them.

In the world of law, the issue of drawing the line is more important. Additionally, consensus is important as a necessary part of the political process. Laws represent social judgments about which individuals or species will receive the protection or consideration of the law, and in which circumstances. It is hoped that all readers of this book, being rational and ethical actors, will agree that chimpanzees, dogs, cats, horses, and dolphins, among others, because of their capacity to experience pain and suffering, should be considered ethical subjects. that is, beings within our ethical universe. It is not the focus of this book to decide where the line should be drawn. What is important is that some animals are ethical subjects; the consequences of acknowledging these animals as ethical subjects are complex enough to fill this book.

It should be noted that much of the argument about where to draw the ethical line identifies human capacities as the measuring bar: self-awareness, consciousness, communication capabilities, and tool-making being some of the presumed critical attributes. This is speciesism at work. Why should human capacities be the measurement of ethical concern for all of life on Earth? We humans for much of our history believed we were at the center of the physical universe. Careful observations by individuals such as Galileo Galilei and Leonardo da Vinci, combined with rational assessment and truth-seeking, showed that our world is but one point in a vast universe of physical objects rotating and expanding in all directions. As special as Earth is to us, it is not a focal point in the broad sweep of our Milky Way galaxy.

Likewise, the next century will probably evolve this view, suggesting that it is neither correct nor useful to place humans at the center of the ethical universe. We may be special, but we are not alone. While humans are the most powerful species on Earth, power does not create ethical status. For example, the sun has greater power (energy) than all humans combined, but it has no ethical status. It is life itself that creates ethical status. Up until recently, humans have simply been part of the wave of life that has flowed and evolved over the eons. Our concern or lack of concern about other beings had little impact on the full scope and movement of life on the planet. The narrowness of our moral universe did not significantly affect the life processes on Earth. While human agriculture has been transforming ecosystems for centuries, in the past fifty or so years the power possessed and exercised by humans has significantly changed the equations.

Returning to the example of Homer above, another critical point to be stated here is that a primary difference between the dog and the ball is that the ball has no inherent interests of its own. Both the dog and the little boy do have interests of their own. That is, the fact of being alive means individuals, self-contained physical beings, have capabilities and preferences. As a consequence of our DNA programing, the two most important preferences are, first, to act to continue life, or self-preservation; second, the will and need to produce the next generation of our species.[3]

The deepest level of DNA programming for all beings sets in motion the possibilities for specific capabilities and preferences to support the goal of reproduction. The goldfish will do everything within its limited power to live and to reproduce; a television will not. The baby rabbit emits a scream as the crow bears her away for dinner. She was not taught to do this; it is a response genetically provided to confuse the predator. If the scream causes her to be dropped, then she can continue to exercise her preference for life. Of course, on the other hand, the crow must eat to exercise its preference for life. Another term for preference is *interest*, and this word will be critical in developing our ethical perspective. The concept of interests as characteristics of living beings will become very important when weighing the competing interests between ethical actors and ethical subjects.

Having established that animals have interests that enter into our ethical considerations does not suggest how much weight such interests should be given when set against the interests of humans or other non-human animals. A few more concepts need to be developed before we address this critical question.

CHAPTER 2

THE FORK IN THE ROAD: THE USE OF BEINGS

Accepting that at least some animals are ethical subjects, how do we move forward, what is the next issue to face? The experiences of a thousand conversations over the decades suggests to me that the most fruitful question to address next is the issue of whether it is acceptable for humans to ever use animals in any way.

The fact that humans do use animals for an extraordinary number of activities, daily food and daily companionship being the most obvious, does not provide an answer to the question of whether we ought to use them. Humans attend horse races, dog races, dogfights, cockfights, and bullfights. Rodeos and circuses have animals integral to the sport and entertainment they present. We use animals that we do not ever see. How many rats, mice, rabbits, and monkeys are used around the world for science and product testing? How many millions of chicken hens are hidden in warehouses for the entirety of their lives to produce the eggs ubiquitously consumed by humans? While not so prevalent today in the United States, how many animals around the world provide labor and transportation for humans or their fur and skin for clothing and shoes? Millions and millions of dogs and cats live with us, enriching and helping our daily lives. Also remember the wildlife, the fish and deer used as food, and the bobcats used by humans for fur trim and coats. Humans have discovered adventure vacations where they travel to visit the mountain gorilla, or the penguins of the Antarctic. Then there are the gangs and warlords of Africa who kill elephants to obtain and sell their ivory to buy the guns and ammunition of war. How many sharks have suffered and been killed for a nutritionally useless shark-fin soup? We use animals all the time; but we seldom think whether we ought to use them, or what conditions should exist before allowing their use.

Given the near-universal use of animals by humans, why even bother to raise such a question? Because a more-extreme group of individuals within the larger animal-rights community has asserted loudly and strongly that any use of an animal, by a human, is unethical; that animals deserve equal consideration with humans; that animals as property are the slaves of humans and such status should be abolished. Indeed, they group themselves together as "abolitionist" (those who seek the abolition of the property status of animals and the elimination of the use of animals by humans).[1] Further, they state that once being freed of the status of property, animals can become legal persons and possess legal rights. While I am in partial agreement with the end point, that some animals can and should become legal persons and possess some legal rights, my path forward to reach this end point is very different.

While the perspectives of the abolitionists are not widely known among the general public, they have captured much of the intellectual energy within the animal-rights movement. I think this energy could be better directed toward enhancing the welfare of animals alive today. Therefore, this chapter seeks to engage those within the animal-rights movement, but it will be helpful for all readers to understand the bricks that form the foundation of my animal ethics. While an alternative grouping of perspectives can be found under the conceptual heading of "animal welfare," these ideas are not rich or complex enough to capture my perspective. The best phrase for my ethical outlook is "respectful use."

Because of the importance of addressing the arguments and concerns of the abolitionists directly, this discussion will be organized, in part, around the premises of their perspective. First, animals, or some subcategory of them, are ethical subjects. We both agree on this point, as per the prior chapter. Second, there is an ethical equality between humans and nonhuman animals (perhaps only a subset of mammals). Third, because the ethical status of animals is similar to that of humans, the legal property status of animals should be eliminated (the evils of the enslavement of humans are like the slavery of animals, since they both arise out of being the property of humans).[2] However, to compare your pet dog to human slavery is insulting to humans and nonsense for the dog. Such a claim significantly ignores the levels of denigration that humans did and do inflict upon other humans when in the position of being masters over human slaves. Dogs are not as complex as humans. While they and we do share the capacity to feel pain and suffer, in my experience they do not have the intellectual and emotional complexity of humans and therefore cannot be as deeply denigrated as a human might be. To support the abolitionist position, you have to believe that to be a companion animal is inherently denigrating for the animal. Such a position is not supported by reality. Yet it does have to be recognized and accepted that a portion of humans do inflict pain and suffering on their dogs and other pets.

Consider the premise of the abolitionists that, since animals and humans are biologically alike, they therefore are beings that are ethically alike as well. This is too simplistic to be helpful. It is not that humans are biologically different in our physical bodies; evolution clearly ties our biology (physiology) together with other animals. We have had that concept before us since the publications of Charles Darwin, including *On the Origin of Species*. Rather, we are different from the other animals in a collective sense based upon the knowledge and physical power humans now possess, which results in the context of a social and economic structure that has given humans the capacity to control or impact vast portions of the earth. Most animals are under our dominion and control whether or not they are our property. The reality of shared evolution is insufficient to support a blanket premise of the nonuse of animals by humans. (For more on this topic, see chapter 13, "We Are the Gods of Old.")

As a counterpoint to the abolitionist approach, a better first step in the analysis is to determine whether there are any circumstances in which it is acceptable for humans to use animals. This is the fork in the road; if you agree that no human should use an animal in any circumstance, then the path of the abolitionist is acceptable. If you agree that at least some use of animals, even if they exist as property, is ethically acceptable, then another path, that of respectful use, is available. To make this determination requires a consideration of what the word "use" might mean.

Is having a pet or a companion animal using the animal? Those within the animal movement prefer the term "companion animal" over that of "pet." Common language use of the term "pet" can have a tone of lack of respect or of being of little concern to the owner or guardian. On the other hand, the term "companion animal" suggests an animal emotionally closer to a human and more respected. The term "companion animal" will be used to designate those animals with which at least one specific human has created an emotional and personal bond.

Returning to the word "use," it is employed so often that its meaning is hard to pin down. Skipping the noun form of the word, our focus is on the use of the verb form. The definition that is most relevant to this discussion is: *to put into service (help, benefit or welfare), especially to attain an end.*[3] Consider the example from the prior chapter, in which Homer enters the house with one of three objects on the floor before him: a ball, a dog, or a child. If he kicks the ball, has he used the ball? Yes, the end or benefit he seeks is emotional release of frustration and negative events. When he kicks the ball, he uses it to obtain an outcome. But, as suggested before, the ball is not an ethical subject, so we have no ethical concern with the act, even if it is a use. If the object is either the child or the dog, since both are ethical subjects, we now do have ethical concerns. The actual use could be any of those previously suggested: step on the dog, kick the dog, yell at the dog, call the dog, pet the dog, or hug the dog. If he either kicks or hugs the dog or the child, he has used either or both of them in seeking an end, whether or not he is conscious of why he does it.

Of course, pets use us all the time; they use us to obtain food, water, and emotional support, to name the obvious. Indeed, the ideal companion-animal relationship is one of mutual respectful use, much like in an ideal marriage. Parents use their children all the time, too; they often use their labor (e.g., for household chores, or animal care) and their love. Recall, here we are focusing on the meaning of "use" as to put something or someone into service, especially to attain an end.

While the word "use" standing alone can be cast in a negative sense (e.g., "He used her to get to the family money."), for our purposes the word simply defines a relationship existing between two ethical beings. (We will ignore the use of inanimate objects in this discussion.) Having found the existence of the relationship of use, the second step is to characterize the use as positive or negative, good or bad. This obviously requires a judgment and the acceptance of some set of values and experiences with which to make the judgments.

Human communities usually condemn the sexual use of children by their parents (or by anyone else, for that matter). Clearly this is a negative use. Why? Experience informs us that beyond the immediate physical pain and injury, the psychological harm to the vulnerable child is significant and long-term. Whatever the benefit of the act for the adult, it does not justify the likely harm to the child. Thus, it is easy to condemn sexual use as an unethical use. Indeed, such acts are serious crimes within the legal system. Likewise, kicking or striking the child in any way will be considered a negative use not justified by the prospective benefit to the ethical actor—in this case, Homer.

What about kicking the dog? While I do not wish to enter into a discussion of the full complexity of a dog's mind, it should be acceptable to state that kicking a dog has not only the immediate consequence of physical pain and harm but psychological harm as well. Whether the psychological harm is identical to that of the child is not relevant here, because the cumulative negative impact clearly outweighs the possible benefits to Homer, making it an unethical act. This is a particularly easy judgment since we also know that if Homer would simply hug the child or the dog, then both parties of the use relationship will receive a benefit of a positive nature, allowing an easy judgment of positive use and therefore ethical conduct.

A more difficult judgment about the quality of the use arises when considering visits to a zoo. The family passing by a live animal exhibit is using the animal for visual entertainment and perhaps, hopefully, self-education. This is a light, short use, lasting perhaps thirty seconds. Is this use justified? Does the benefit to the human family justify the confinement of the animal at the zoo? Such confinement does not (usually) cause direct pain and suffering to the animal. How much of an interference with the life needs of the animal that the confinement represents will depend upon the animal and the level of care she receives. If a chimpanzee is the animal at the zoo, then the risk of negative consequences is higher than if the animal being kept is a snake. The chimpanzee possesses a more complex brain, which supports the presence of more complex capacities. Confinement is more likely to be negative as more interests or capacities of the animal can be frustrated. Besides the species, the other information needed is exactly how the animal is confined and treated, but this is usually hard to judge as one walks by an exhibit. It is a clear and easy judgment that no animal should be confined for life so that one family of humans can be entertained. But then, what if over the lifetime of the animal a million humans pass by, and a hundred of them change the focus of their lives to protect and care about the species as a result of viewing the exhibit? Now the calculus becomes complex.

I have seen some exhibits of chimpanzees where, in my judgment, the conditions were ethically acceptable, and those where it was ethically unacceptable. A premise of this judgment is that the chimpanzee had to live somewhere or be killed. It would not be ethical in my view to capture a chimpanzee in the wild and bring him to a US zoo no matter how nice the facility. Part of the consideration will have to be: If the chimpanzee was not in the zoo, providing entertainment, then where would he be? Would the lives of chimpanzees be better or worse in the alternative locations? Whether or not humans should use chimpanzees for breeding is a separate ethical question; here we are focused on the simple use of them as exhibits for human visual entertainment.

Many fact patterns are in the gray area. But if a given chimpanzee were born in the United States, there are places where the use of the chimpanzee is ethically acceptable. It does us no good to argue at the moment about where to draw the line; the point is that the use may be either positive or negative. That it is difficult to draw a line does not negate the reality of positive fact patterns; however, it does suggest that there is an enhanced risk of abuse by those whose actions are not careful or concerned about seeking only positive ethical outcomes for the human use of animals. This is why the law must be part of the conversation. The law will seek to control the actions of humans who either don't understand or reject the need for positive ethical outcomes as being a basis for animal use.

> **A use is not inherently an abuse.**

If the reader can accept the proposition that some uses of animals are ethically positive, then the position of the abolitionist should be rejected. So the fork in the road is chosen. But, if the reader is uncertain, a decision does not have to be made yet; there are many pages of consideration about just where the path of respectful use will take us. Perhaps a more-detailed consideration of the destination will make the choice of the fork easier. Just what might respectful use entail?

CHAPTER 3

RESPECTFUL USE

Ⅰf we accept that at least some animals are ethical subjects that may be used by humans, even as they remain within some version of the property-law system, the critical question that must be faced is, which uses are acceptable and which are not? My determination is that it is an acceptable use if it is a respectful use.

What is respect? The power of the concept was crystalized in the song "Respect," sung by Aretha Franklin in 1967. While the song never exactly says what the word might mean, it was an anthem for the women's movement of the time. Everyone thought they knew what she meant and agreed she should get it. And we men knew what she meant and that she was right. Husbands should show respect for their wives, when either he comes home or when she comes home. If marriage is to last, it must be supported with respect.

At its core, showing respect consists of several components. The first is an acknowledgment of the presence of another being as part of your world and that you need to interact with this individual in a particular way. The focus here is on the verb in question. He hit the dog; he hugs the dog; he respects the dog. The dictionary says that respect means *to consider worth of high regard, to have concern for, to refrain from interfering with*; "respect implies a considered evaluation or estimation."[1] It is disrespectful not to show regard or concern for another. Respect is not how you act, but rather how you feel, or what you believe, which will, in turn, cause you to act in a particular way. For instance, "Alfred never talks back to his mother; he is respectful of her." While this may be an outward manifestation of respect, it may or may not be motivated by internal respect. Alfred may engage in respectful acts out of fear of being beaten with a belt.

"Respect," as it will be used in this book, is an individual's judgment or state of mind that produces a belief that may result in actions or inactions in regard to another individual. This process may or may not be controlled or understood by the conscious part of the brain. Consider how this may play out in your daily life: It is a wet night, at dusk; you pull up at a stop sign and notice movement on the edge of the road. It is a small wet mound of fur, a cat perhaps. You put the car in park, get out, and pick up the wet bundle and put it your car. You have shown respect for the cat, her life does matter.

Respect is a state of mind that arises because of a specific capacity for complex judgments within the brain (see chapter 10, "The Process of Making Judgments"). This capacity is a judgment not about external facts like sound and color but about the state of affairs within an individual's brain regarding relationships with others. Respect is not an on/off, black-or-white option. Rather, respectfulness can be projected on a continuum, moving from slightly respectful to highly respectful. Moving along this continuum to greater respect will result in the ethical actor giving increasing weight to the interests and needs of the ethical subject—the animal or child. And, of course, just to make it more difficult, this process has no physical attribute. It is the sum of our experiences and reasoning, shaped by the neuron network within a particular human mind. When we have or seek positive relationships with others, we have respect for them. This book seeks to expand our awareness that "others" can and should encompass nonhuman beings.

As a quick legal aside, "respect" is not a word found within the law, but the requirements of humane treatment for animals does arise out of a societal respect. There are no laws specifically requiring respect, because it is almost impossible to truly understand what thoughts or emotions exist within a specific human head. And it is not possible to define the word with legal precision. Also, the law is not really certain who should be respected.

However, the law may feel comfortable in seeking to control disrespectful acts, such as the stealing of a cat from a human or the kicking of a dog. The law may also promote respectful acts such as, the making of charitable contributions to soup kitchens and humane societies. In this sense, the law reflects the difference between promoting acts and holding beliefs.

How does this sense of high regard come to exist within an individual's mind? One path is when the other being represents a threat to you, to your physical well-being. To stand on the plains of Africa's Serengeti in the presence of a group of young male elephants, with local escorts who have only a spear to protect the visitor, will cause the human there to have a respect for those amazing beings. This will not necessarily happen when seeing an elephant in a zoo, behind all those thick steel bars. Respect is an acknowledgment of the presence of another who has the capacity to impose his will upon us. This is respect arising out of the motivation for self-preservation and a capacity to understand the risk before us. On my farm, the younger rams acknowledge the presence of the senior ram, move out of his way, and are almost courteous to him; they show and feel respect. My cats are respectful of Annie, my large Great Pyrenees dog, perhaps with the respect flowing into fearfulness.

But of course, respect out of personal fear is not really the focus of our discussion, since we ethical beings seldom are in the presence of animals we fear. Rather, it is when we seek to act, or not, and it is foreseeable that the action will have an impact on this other being about whom we have a threshold of concern. Returning to the story about Homer, when he opens the door and makes a decision about what to do next, it would be disrespectful to inflict pain on the dog. It would be respectful to hug the dog.

Respect is the internal acknowledgment of another being who is deserving of your time, attention, and resources. It is a socially attractive force that is critical to holding our social structure together. The degrees of respect, which exist within someone's mind, create the differing levels of ethical obligations that arise within the same mind. (See figures 3.1 and 3.2 at end of this chapter.) Respect is changeable, as new information is gained, and values may change with life's experiences. Who might be deserving of respect is a social as well as an internal conversation. Choose three people you know and ask yourself: Do I respect them, how much do I respect them, and why do I do so? Do you respect your companion animal? How about the animals at the zoo?

Now, as I will do a number of times in this book, a consideration of children will be touched upon to provide some context before a detailed consideration of animals. This is not to suggest that animals are morally equal to human children, but rather that children are beings who are living their lives in the ignorance of the concerns of ethics or law and who cannot advocate for themselves within our adult world. Is it ethically acceptable for a couple to use the labor of their children? Yes, usually. Much of human history finds that children have been used by their family to support the family with their labor. The child's labor can be an important asset of a human family. Such use may be respectful or disrespectful. How many farmers and ranchers historically and today depend upon their children to make the farms and ranches economically viable? Additionally, it is often through the imposition of labor and the responsibilities placed by parents upon their children that the human values of a family are transmitted from one generation to the next. This might include acceptance of responsibility, pride in work, the need to work, self-reliance, and the confidence needed to accomplish tasks.

Can the use of children become ethically unacceptable outside the home, in other words, disrespectful? Yes. In the early 1900s children were taken out of school, often kept in unhealthy and unsafe working conditions. Working ten-hour days for six or seven days a week is too much use. It does not allow the child to be educated, receive healthcare, or develop those characteristics that are important to them as individuals in the realization of their potential. Historically, when industry had possession and control of a child, and the primary goal was the making of money, clearly some abused that position of power. There had to be some lines drawn by society to protect the children from abusive parents or abusive jobs. The risk of abuse by business is deemed so high that our society has adopted laws to prohibit the use of children under a certain age, in most circumstances.[2]

Does the real likelihood of abuse of some children require the conclusion that there should be no children born at all because some may be abused? No. Society has the duty to reduce the risk of abuse, and it must be acknowledged that, notwithstanding our best efforts, some abuse still exists. Likewise, the risk of abuse of animals by humans does not support the conclusion that there should be no domestic use of animals. It must be acknowledged that the risk of abuse of animals by humans is significantly higher for animals than it is for children, particularly for agricultural animals where human owners (corporations) are primarily focused on the desire for economic profit. Additionally, whereas the farmer of one hundred years ago knew, and often respected, the individual animals on the farm, today the shareholder and officers of the corporations seldom, if ever, see or touch the animals they own. Commercial animals often are not considered as individuals but are viewed as just a bunch of inventory to be used to make products like chicken salad or soup. In such circumstances there is a high risk of disrespectful use.

The following poem is one of a number written by me and sprinkled throughout the book. They are a break in the flow of the chapter, a moment to pause and consider something a little different. They deal with the human relationship with animals specifically, or the human relationship with the environment, or simply about being human. Now, you might ask: why is he dragging environmental issues into a book about relationships with individual animals? This is because the ultimate abstraction of showing respect for animals is the showing respect for the planet that holds the entirety of all living beings we know. We must respect the home of others, be they human or animal. Okay, you say, but why any focus on humans? We often forget, or set on the side, the reality that humans are animals, and therefore to the extent we can learn about ourselves, we can learn about the nonhuman animals as well.

RESPECTING ANIMALS

An Ethical Compass

Do you have a
Compass?
Inside your
Mind?

Which way will
You go?
With Animals?

Do you care
Enough?
To learn about
Animals?
To work for
Animals?
To support
Animals?

Do they care?
About what?

Can you show
Them,
Respect?

Someone might believe that his or her use of an animal is respectful, while others might disagree. For example, is it respectful of a cat to have her claws removed? If the cat's claws are removed, then the human has the benefits of a reduced risk of modest harm or discomfort to themselves, their children, and the furniture. The removal for the cat is like a human losing the first joint of each finger. Yes, the cat can continue with life, but he or she is without a physical attribute fairly important to the cat. In my judgment, claw removal is not a respectful act to perform on a cat. Indeed, the cutting off of any body part of a dog or cat seems disrespectful. However, if the removal of claws is the only option for the cat to continue to have life, it is better to have life without claws than to have the death of the cat. This also requires the cat owner to recognize that a declawed cat places on the owner a special obligation to safeguard and protect the cat from potential danger in which the cat normally would be expected to protect itself but would not be able to.

Another example is dogfighting. Is the putting of a dog into a ring in the presence of another fighting dog, with the anticipation of perhaps a fight to the death, a respectful use of the dogs? It is not clear that humans who fight dogs see the dogs as "other beings" with their own interests. If this were the case, then dogfighting is not an ethical decision to that person. In the mind of these humans, their interests in gaining money, prestige, and other rewards obviously outweigh any consideration of the extreme pain and suffering imposed upon their dogs. But in this case the consequences to the dog are so horrific that society has decided, through the law-making process, that the use of dogs for fighting is so disrespectful that it must be considered criminal activity. This judgment is reflected in the federal and state laws that make dogfighting, the supporting dogfighting, or possessing fighting dogs a serious crime.[3] Society, through the adoption of laws, can block or deter disrespectful acts, regardless of personal judgments. The same judgment has also been reached on the issue of cockfighting.

The reader might have noticed that I have not offered a formula for how much weight to allot to the interests of an animal when a human makes a "use decision" about an animal. This is not possible. Ethical decisions are personal and complex decisions not subject to fixed formulas. Some issues, like dogfighting and cockfighting, are so obvious that delicate balancing is not necessary. However, there are some signposts to help a person judge whether ethically acceptable, respectful use is occurring.

The threshold is crossed when an individual realizes the appropriateness and necessity of engaging in the balancing of one's conflicting interests with that of an animal. One can hypothesize that humans engaged in dogfighting do not pass this threshold. A person who decides whether or not to declaw a household cat may or may not have crossed that threshold. That is, either it is not an ethical decision in the person's mind, or it is an ethical decision that can have a yes or no outcome.

A second step occurs when the keeper of the animal seeks out information about the animal, both the nature of the species and the characteristics of the individual animal with which the person is dealing. Does the cat keeper understand what is entailed in the declawing operation itself and what the lifelong impact on the cat's behavior and capacity will be? Will the cat be going outside? Will she need to protect herself?

The third test of the presence of respectful use is whether or not the individual human, in fact, changes his or her conduct to accommodate the interests of the animal. If the human interests always win, then it is not working. The cheapest and easiest way to take a four-day, pet-free, weekend trip if you have a pet cat or dog is to put a bucket of water and an open bag of dried food in a room of your house or apartment. Then just put the animal in the room and close the door. More than likely the animal will be alive when the human returns, but somehow this does not seem to be a respectful form of care of the pet. It will take time and money to find a pet-sitter or a good kennel, but that is what respectful use requires. The issue is not what is legal or illegal. It is what is ethical and what is unethical.

The fourth test, an objective test, is to look at the animal in question and observe whether or not she is a healthy, well-adjusted, and socially balanced animal. A dog on a tether for twelve hours a day is not being treated respectfully, and more than likely the dog will not be healthy, well-adjusted, or socially balanced. A horse may be used to pull a wagon, but the continuing health of the horse should be a primary concern of the owner, not just the money generated by horse's labor. If money becomes more important, the objective evidence of the failure to realize a proper balance will be found in observing the well-being of the horse herself.

In such a case the use of the horse may have moved from respectful to disrespectful.

What if the wagon-pulling horse is clearly not in good health? There are no ethics police to call. If physical conditions slide far enough, then a violation of the criminal law relating to the humane treatment of animals may occur, but our ethical standards often demand more than the law may require. The only real option for an outsider is to try to engage the owner/keeper of the animal in dialogue, to have a conversation about the horse, what might be done differently, and why the horse matters. Ethical conduct arises out of self-enlightenment. Sometimes others can aid in the process of realization of self-enlightenment, but not always.

Those humans who are classified as hoarders of animals represent a particularly difficult case. This may be the case when a sixty-year-old woman is found to have eighty cats in her suburban home. The house is a mess and the cats are not being cared for, yet the woman is in denial about the conditions being faced by the cats. Such a person may well agree that animals should be respected and believe deeply that she does respect her animals. But such a person is unable to engage in the respectful acts that ought to follow. There is a significant disconnect between the person's subjective beliefs and the objective disrespectful conditions that the animals actually live in. A hoarder has lost the mental capacity to transform beliefs into action or to understand what action needs to be taken. The only real remedy is to separate the human from the animals and to provide support and treatment for both. Sending a hoarder to jail is disrespectful of the human.

One final point to consider is how the likelihood of respect is increased when the human being is in physical and visual contact with the animal in question. The likelihood that respect will arise within a specific human mind is greater the more the human personally sees, interacts, and perhaps touches a specific animal. It is more likely that Homer will be respectful of his dog than that the family at the zoo will be respectful of the animals they observe. If there is a separation of ownership and keeper of an animal, then respectful attitudes are even more difficult to generate. If the owner is separated from the animal and the use (death) of the animal makes money for the owner, it is a third level away from respectful use. Consider the racehorse that is never seen by the 10 percent owner who lives three states away, compared to the groom who cares for the horse every day. But it is the owner, not the groom, who controls the future of the horse. Consider shareholders of the megacorporations who own farms of chickens intended for slaughter. The owners of the chickens, the shareholders, are usually not aware of the existence of individual animals, let alone do they have a respectful relationship with these creatures.

Respect has a strong emotional component that is triggered by the individuality of an animal with which the human shares some space. However, once a human respects a specific animal, and understands that respect, it becomes a relatively easy task to project that respect to other, perhaps unseen, animals. In such a case the human draws an analogy between the animal he or she knows directly and those that are not known so intimately.

Respect is a core concept or state of mind when developing an ethic by an individual human and the creation of internal, self-imposed limitations of action by that individual. Respect may be a motivation for political action and legal change, but no law can make one person respect another being. The law may set up social conditions and expectations that trigger self-examination, which in turn could result in respect. It is illegal to discriminate in hiring individuals on the basis of race. This should be a trigger for individuals to ask themselves, "Well, why is it illegal?"

Show a little respect.

> Should dogs and cats have moral rights because we love them, because they love us, or for some other reason?

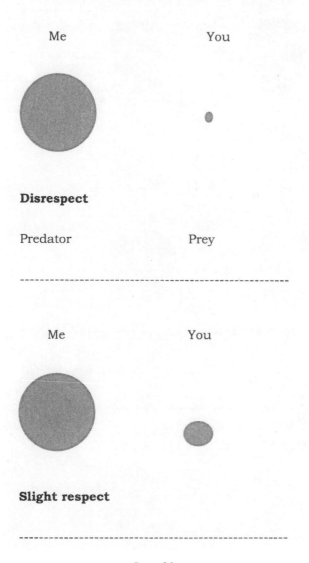

Figure 3.1.

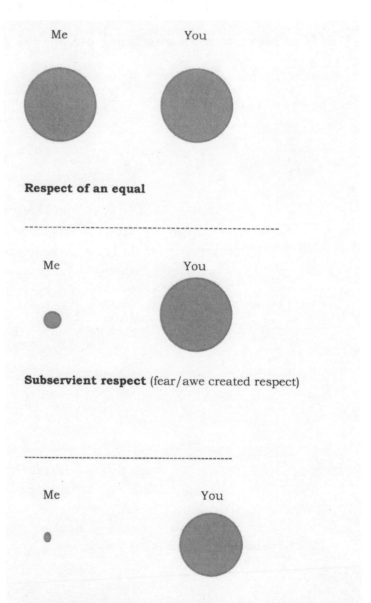

Respect of an equal

Subservient respect (fear/awe created respect)

No self-respect – mentally unstable/unhealthy condition

Figure 3.2.

Each person may have different relationships with other humans and animals, and most of us have a mixture of the above options.

A POSTSCRIPT

This chapter is about the nature of respect as an intellectual, neurological capacity existing within our brains. Perhaps a few words about why this capacity exists would be useful as well. The human animal has any number of biological capacities. We see in color, we hear within a specific range of sound frequencies, we have the capacity for word recognition and language that relates to a specific site within the brain.[4] More abstractly, we can think about and plan for the future; we are wired to be curious and, at a higher level, to ask that extraordinary question, "Why?" For instance, my sheep are curious but I don't think they can ask themselves, "Why is this happening?" All of these capacities exist as a result of them being positive attributes for the evolutionary survival of the individual humans who compose our species.

As one of the few social species of animals, our capacity to form multigenerational groups, which operate as social groups, was critical in the evolution of the human species. What are the bonds that allow for the creation of groups or communities of humans? This is a book topic in and of itself. Let me just suggest as a hypothesis that while the family shared genes, being bonded by love is critical to social-group cohesion. The genetic evolution that has given us the capacity for creating respect has also been a major factor or characteristic for successful biological survival as social groups, thus supporting the idea of group selection in the forces of evolution. In the absence of direct genetic relationships between individuals, such as mother and daughter, a person can nevertheless decide with whom to work or not work through judgments of respect and disrespect. Respect provides a capacity by which an individual sorts the world for humans fit for association.

RESPECTING ANIMALS

It is a capacity of our brain, a higher level of abstraction not present in most animals, which arose out of positive evolutionary feedback. Respect is not particularly integrated with our language center. That is, even though we certainly can talk about respect, the actual judgment or decision of whom to respect and how much weight to give to that respect for a particular person usually occurs outside either the word center or the sentence-driven consciousness of our mind.

The importance of this capacity is suggested for early humans who formed social groups that were not genetically related. Respect can be the glue that holds together a group of humans even if they are not related. Even in related groups of humans, for a group to function together there must be respect between the leaders and the followers. Does an individual have respect for the leader of his group? Was he willing to do his or her bidding: to build the fire, to go to war, or to collect the fruit for the group? Respect creates emotionally supported positive or negative relationships between individuals. These are judgments of the moment and subject to change as more information is provided to an individual brain. The capacity to form a judgement of respect is fundamental to being human.

CHAPTER 4

THE PROPERTY STATUS

The property status of animals needs to be briefly discussed at this point because of existing attitudes and beliefs of the animal abolitionists, those who believe that all animals merit full personhood in the legal system. One of the premises of the abolitionist worldview is that the reality of animals being the personal property of humans is demeaning to the animals; it is viewed as the equivalent of being animal slaves to humans, and that their freedom from this legal status is required before animals can receive their due legal rights. Whether the property status is demeaning to the animals is discussed below. Some discussion of property law will be useful at this point.

Property law is a set of socially adopted rules that provide social stability by describing the rights and obligations that exist when a person owns property: real, personal, or intellectual property. A significant subpart of property law is the rules that relate to obtaining and transferring the ownership of an item. If you presently have a sheep or a cat and are the sole owner of the animal in the eyes of the law, then you can transfer ownership to another human by gift, sale, or bequest in your will. If your sheep or cat is female and gives birth to a set of lambs or kittens, the law awards ownership of offspring to the owner of the mother.[1]

Property law is admittedly primarily focused on human-to-human rights and responsibilities. The law does not usually say much about the property, the animal, or obligations toward the animal. The general property rule is that, if you own personal property—say, a chair—you may do what you want with it: sit on it, throw it, chop it up, burn it, abandon it, or give it to someone. But here is the first important legal point: if the personal property is an animal, say, a kitten, you may not do anything you want to or with the kitten. The restrictions are within not properly law but criminal law, as articulated in the criminal anti-cruelty laws of each of our states. It is a felony violation almost everywhere in the United States if the owner of a cat burns or abandons the cat. This distinction suggests that law, not just property law, already acknowledges that at least some animals are different from chairs. There is no such thing as a "chair anti-cruelty law." We see this reflected in our language, as well; the cat is considered not an "it," as might be appropriate for most personal property, but a "she" or a "he."

My next book will present a detailed argument for and vision of a changed legal concept of property law for the betterment of animals. Everyone within the animal-rights movement agrees that having dogs and cats in the property category of personal property, along with cars, chairs, and balls, is not helpful to the animals. An alternative to not being property at all is a new category, "living property," for which new policy considerations can develop new rules about the relationships between owners, other humans, and the animals themselves. No one knows what will be the status of animals in our legal system in two hundred years, but it is highly unlikely that the next change for domestic animals will be the elimination of their status in the world of property, as proposed by the abolitionist.

When the new category of living property is created, a fresh consideration of some very old property rules will be appropriate. For example, an important attribute of personal property law is that the owner has the power to sell the property and reap the economic value of the animals. What if a new rule regarding the sale of animals were proposed? The owner of a cat would not be allowed to sell the cat, but could transfer ownership by gift (adoption) or by will at the owner's death. There are interesting and important policy arguments on both sides of that possible rule. To start this discussion, we could begin with, say, cat ownership but leave sheep ownership for another day. Rules could differ by species or community. This would allow maximum opportunity for incremental improvement for the status of animals in the legal system. The creation of a new category, living property, also allows the continuation of the existing rules for humans owning inanimate personal property. Also, before you object and want to talk about the commercial value of your sheep, note that it will be perfectly acceptable to limit a rule to a species such as domestic cats and not to apply it to the honorable category of sheep.

But to the more-critical point, does keeping animals in any property status prohibit them from having legal rights? No. Who may hold legal rights is a social judgment, not a fixed law of the universe. Indeed, a fair case can be made that some animals have some minor legal rights within our present legal structure even though they are personal property (see chapter 16, "A Foray into the Law"). The possibility of legal rights for animals is expanded greatly by moving animals to their own subcategory of property.

Turning to the other point of the abolitionist: animals are diminished by being property. This statement is not meaningful. The human-designated status of property is not loathed by the animals within the human community. The property status of an animal does not demean the animal in his own sense of self, such as that could be determined. While physical space is important for animals, I do not think the sense of personal liberty of movement is nearly as important to animals as it is to humans. What causes them harm is not the property status but the disrespectful use of animals by some owners. Neither the dog nor the rooster complains about being property. It is a concept beyond the grasp of animals. The concept of property is a human construct created to allow animals to become part of various human communities.

There is a risk of a bad, disrespectful relationship for an animal in a property relationship. But consider that the rites of human marriage create a human relationship that contains within it the risk of a bad outcome as well. This outcome is inherent in the creation of the relationship. Does the risk of things going wrong demand that the availability of the relationship for everyone be denied? Perhaps we need to institute preconditions for allowing the relationship to be created rather than denying the possibility of the relationship. Further, there will need to be procedures and rules for when the relationship goes bad. Humans can ask for a divorce, but at the moment animals cannot.

Let me share with you a "conversation" I had a number of years ago, one that set me on the path being pursued today in this book:

THE JET DISCUSSION

It was a brisk fall day when I decided to put some questions to Jet, a ram born on our farm the year before. A mellow ram, he was more approachable than some of the others. In fact, the two of us had often talked football as I scratched his neck and back. He was polite enough not to disagree with most of my keen observations, but he did express a strong preference for the Rams over my favorites, the Lions. We got along, as typical guys talking sports. After the usual pleasantries, I looked him in the eye and put the question to him:

"Do you feel oppressed? Are you troubled by your status as property?"

Jet looked at me with his thoughtful eyes as if to say, "No, I had not noticed that I was property. What does that mean? And 'oppressed.' . . . Well, last night you would not let me into the north pasture, where I wanted some new grass, but I think that is being frustrated, not oppressed. In fact, I have been worried that you and your wife are feeling oppressed by all the obligations you have on our behalf. Marty hauls water for us every day and moves the electric fences for new pasture. On the weekends I see you building shelters and feeders and planting new pasture for us. Two weeks ago, I saw you store two hundred bales of hay in the barn for the winter. All we do is eat, drink, chew our cud, and watch the lady ewes. I hope that our demands are not too much for you, because I like our life."

Then I said, "Well, that's an enlightened view for a young ram. And, don't worry, the work is worth it to us. We will continue to work for you as required. But what about the fact that we take your wool from you? It's not a pleasant process, twenty minutes of being held at awkward angles, and an occasional nick of the skin."

But the ram was not concerned and looked at me as if to comment: "You forget that we pretty much live in the moment. Once it's over, I don't dwell on it. Believe me, getting rid of the blanket is liberation. The only problem is that it's hard to remember who is who when suddenly everyone is naked."

"Well, that's a relief," I replied, and then I sought to pose just one more question. "This is a little abstract for a ram, but give it a shot. Do you believe that the world would be better off if you and your mothers and sisters did not exist, so that humans would be free from the status of being oppressors of animals?"

I could swear Jet looked at me with a strange expression that seemed to suggest, "You're kidding me, right? Get a life! Just because you have psychological issues doesn't mean I don't appreciate being alive."

His glance into my eyes crystallized the answer. It is better to exist as part of the human world, even as property, than to not exist at all. Having shown me this truth, Jet wandered away to find some grass.

From the animal's perspective, a key benefit of being property is that there is a specific human or human substitute who is responsible for his or her care. Under the laws of every state, the owner or keeper of an animal has a duty of care for the animal that is set out in the criminal laws of that state. Under our present legal system, full responsibility comes with ownership. Most animals within the domestic control of humans are not capable of self-care, regardless of their age, and, if released or abandoned by their human owner, they would find themselves in an environment hostile to their existence. (Admittedly, some dogs and cats do and could survive as feral animals, but that raises issues not pursued here.) If domestic animals are not some form of property, then there will be no domestic animals, no companion animals, no food animals—no animals except those that can exist outside our possession and control.

Therefore, at present, legal ownership needs to continue to exist so that responsibility for the care of the domestic animal can be squarely placed on a specific human or group of humans. Of course, this responsibility is broader than just a duty of care toward the animal. Owners are also responsible for bodily injuries or property damage caused by the animals they own.

While a logic loop might be involved with the next thought, it should be set on the table. Without the property-law construct, humans would not be willing or able to support the birth of new generations of domestic animals. Property law allows humans to realize the different values that domestic animals represent to them, thus creating the incentive to support a next generation of animals. These values can be emotional, spiritual, physiological, or monetary.

The abolitionist might say: "That is correct; property law promotes more domestic animals, which is a horrible outcome as animal slaves will be abused and killed by humans." Therefore, they would say, we need to eliminate the property status as an option for creating animal/human relationships.[2] What do you think? Clearly, at present, many animals are abused and killed by humans. Should that reality drive a stake in the heart of a property law that allows a relationship between specific humans and specific animals? Do more animals win or lose by being part of a property relationship? The answer to that question will vary greatly depending upon which human-animal community is considered. In the area of animal companions, most animals are winners; in the area of industrial agriculture, most animals are losers. What of animals raised for their fur, such as minks or chinchillas? What about animals in zoos or those in the entertainment industry?

Another perspective, more practical in nature, is that viewing animals as property is a social construct that simply is not going away any time soon. Domestic animals are ingrained in our society at such a level that anyone proposing elimination of domestic animals to a legislature will not be taken seriously. If there is a desire to help the animals among us and the future generations of animals, the existence of property relations with animals has to be accepted as a given. Now, that does not mean that particular legal rules cannot be changed. No, it does not. Property law has a great capacity to change, to evolve as society changes or evolves.

That's enough of law for the present. It's time now to turn back to ethics.

> For domestic animal, first there must be life, then liberty.

INTERLUDE: FENCE ROW FARM

Although our genetic heritage is our starting point, we are what we have made of our journey of life. Until 1997, my wife, Marty, and I had a life journey that was very ordinary in a number of ways. We both grew up in typical American suburbs with our respective families. We started our marriage while I was in law school and we were living in the back half of an old farmhouse surrounded by cornfields. When we left that home neither of us had any idea we might someday own a cornfield. After graduation, as I moved from the practice of law to the teaching of law, we moved through four different houses in subdivisions of Virginia and Michigan. When the law school that has employed me since 1977 moved from downtown Detroit to Michigan State University in East Lansing, we saw an opportunity to fulfill a dream: to escape the suburbs and buy a little land. After an amazing string of improbable events, we ended up owning a 100-acre row farm southwest of the university.

When we purchased it, the parcel had 67 acres of row crops, 27 acres of woods, and an abandoned 5-acre field that was made up of weeds rather than a meadow. A tree-lined lane split the rectangle lengthwise, from the west side (with the house and barns on the west side) to the back woods, a half a mile to the east. We live off a public dirt road. The back side of a 400-acre farm is across this road, preserving a perfect setting for amazing sunsets. Our neighbor uses horses to plant and harvest his fields. The west side of our neighbor's farm across the road is a small river/creek that is summer home for numerous birds, including Canadian geese and Sandhill cranes. They provide a sound landscape during the fall as they fly over our land, preparing for migration. Sometimes we hear the beating of their wings; other times they are high in the sky, but always honking back and forth, in the joy of life.

Resting at the lip of this modest river valley, we have gently sloping land. Maple and walnut trees of eighty-plus years line both the public road and the edges of our property; the south side is bounded by an abandoned railroad track and a very occasional stream from snow and spring rain. In the summer, no other house is visible from ours. In the winter, when the maples and walnuts have dropped their covering leaves, the twinkling lights of our neighbor farms remind us that we are not entirely alone.

In Michigan, roads usually have been placed along existing land-survey lines, so that we are part of a one-mile square. For our square, there are no houses or roads except on the edges; the interior of the square consists of cropland, woods, or pasture. The rectangle of our land pushes into the center of the human-free square.

The impact of the land on our quality of life may be obscure to many—certainly to the young who seek out the energy and vitality of the peopled city life. As you walk on our land, away from the house and barns toward the center of the square, you dip in to a soothing silence that with time brings restfulness to the soul. In the summer and fall, a quiet wind through the leaves provides a natural low background sound. It is generally so quiet that you can hear the tire noise of one car half a mile away; an airplane occasionally breaks the silence on its way from Detroit to Chicago. But there are many moments when no human-generated sound can be heard, and you are in a private wilderness. In the fields after a snowstorm, the silence is complete. How many people have experienced the delicate beauty of new patterns of snow, observed in complete silence? We know we are lucky, that few have the opportunity to live this rural life.

Shortly after moving onto the farm, I stepped down as dean of the law school, and one of the staff members who knew me fairly well gave me a book to read, Gene Logson's *The Contrary Farmer*. It suggested an entirely new perspective on the agricultural industry of which we were now a part; it suggested all was not well with big machines and high capital investments. Other books followed, and then we discovered a monthly newspaper, the *Stockman Grass Farmer*, edited by H. Allan Nation. Again, it suggested a different vision, one of agricultural animals on grass: healthy for the animals, healthy for the humans, and much better for the environment.

When we first owned the farm, we leased out the land to a big equipment farmer who rotated corn and soybeans with occasional crops of wheat. The growing crops were beautiful and the farming equipment impressive, but the land lay naked most of the year, subject to erosion and unusable by us. After ten years, we did not renew the lease. Instead, we decided to plant pasture and grasses over all the crop fields. We cleaned our land palette of the chemicals of commercial crops and have sought to establish a living, breathing soil with pasture plants.

As our youngest child set her sights on college, my wife's eyes roamed over all the land and decided that we needed animals. In her mind was a vision of the ideal family farm, the classic Old MacDonald's farm. One summer, before our daughter departed, we tried keeping horses, and while my wife enjoyed their presence and their soft muzzles, they seemed big and dangerous to me. Our daughter liked the idea of horses but was not so taken with their daily requirements. So we returned them to their owners. While Marty was contemplating the merits of goats, a friend urged us to come see some sheep that she had bought. The next day, we attended the Michigan Fiber Festival in Allegan, Michigan, to see her new Icelandic sheep. Visiting the exhibit, we were struck with their beauty, with their long, multicolored fleeces and the impressive horns of the rams. Their eyes had a clarity and focus that was different from other sheep. Months passed by, some fences were built, and we became the proud possessors of a flock of four sheep. Now, a few years later, we started showing our sheep at the same festival, allowing others to discover their beauty. Somehow the four turned into thirty, then sixty, and with the arrival of the new lambs, perhaps eighty amazing sheep. Icelandic chickens appeared one day; another day brought some llamas. Of course we needed Great Pyrenees to help guard the sheep; and the cats just show up, looking for food and shelter.

Dealing with the sheep on our land has shaped my vision of the human-animal future. They are not pets, but they have names. They do not have emotional attachments to us like our dogs or cats, but they are dependent upon us. The rams like back rubs and head rubs, but most of the ladies stay just out of my reach. They are not from a line of predators (like dogs and cats) but are prey species and, as such, view the world differently. I have looked them in their eyes, on beautiful summer days and in snowstorms when they decide to stay outside and are covered with white. I believe their life is good, worth living, and that the family farm of multiple species is an ethical and environmental positive. Living this way has given me an experience and an understanding that was impossible in the suburbs or a city. It has recast my outlook and allowed a complex ethic to develop. I think it useful to share this view of animal/human relationships with those who have not had the opportunities that I have. I will come back a number of times to the role of the farm in my vision of the future world.

CHAPTER 5

INTRODUCTION TO COMMUNITIES

Accepting as a premise that humans have some ethical obligations toward animals, and that animals will be respectfully used by humans, then the question to be addressed is, What is the extent of that obligation? Here again, the abolitionists, those who view animals that are in a property status as being slaves, have sought to establish a premise of thought that is not helpful. The premise is that a rabbit, whether located in the field, in a home, in a barn, or in a research lab, is the same creature (which is true biologically) and therefore must be treated the same in all human contexts.[1] On the surface this is logical, but it is too simplistic to deal with the ethical dilemmas that must be considered.

One of the premises of this book is that animals should not expect better treatment, ethically or legally, than humans receive. So, it will be important to consider the issue of equality of ethical treatment in the human context as well as in the animal context. While at a biological level all humans are about the same, does it follow that we have identical ethical obligations to all humans? While superficial logic suggests yes, the real answer is no. Ethical obligations and rights arise not from simply being human but out of the nature of the shared communities that other humans inhabit with us. A relationship with my daughter is different from that with a neighbor because one is within the community of family and the other is not. Your relationship with someone at work is different from that with a stranger in a distant city, and in turn that is different from the relationship with someone in a different part of the world.

RESPECTING ANIMALS

Equal consideration for all humans, while perhaps an appropriate general statement of principle, is not the reality within my mind, or that of our legal system. Whom would I die for? Whom would I spend time helping? Whom would I spend money helping? Understanding the vision of this book means distinguishing between the absolutes of logic and the realities experienced by individuals. It is the latter that is my concern. Ethics do not arise out of the mere existence of two ethically relevant beings, but by the nature of the relationship between them. (I do acknowledge that there is a core set of ethical principles that apply to all persons irrespective of their relationship to me or whether or not I know them. This arises out of them simply being human: killing without just cause is wrong, torture is wrong, taking something from someone without permission is wrong, physical and verbal abuse of another person is wrong, etc.) It is not clear that there is a core set of principles that humans acknowledge are owed to animals.

One measure of the usefulness of a theory is to understand the boundaries of the theory.[2] Narrow boundaries result in narrow, less useful, theories. The boundary of the discussion of animals by the abolitionist is defined by a comparison of individual humans and individual animals. For example, say that a boy and pig are in a sinking boat; the water is running in, so which one do you save? If a teenage girl and a chimpanzee are sitting in a room, what is the difference between the two that gives the girl full legal rights and chimpanzee none? When one compares the physical makeup of the girl or boy—their bone and muscle and neurological system, which produces and realizes pain—the differences with the pig and the chimpanzee are modest, but admittedly the human brain has capabilities that the pig and the chimpanzee brains do not. I agree that the differences do not justify the human having all the rights and the nonhuman receiving no rights. However, this is just a first-level analysis. There are more complex levels to consider. Their theory of equality is bounded by, and limited by, having only a biological comparison of individuals.[3]

But the nature of humans is not just defined by individual biological entities and the capabilities and characteristics of a single human body. As our species evolved over the past 100,000 years, there were no ethical or legal concerns about the treatment of animals, for at that time in evolution there was no human society that possessed the ethical or legal concerns of today. Humans survived and expanded with the intertwining combination of genetic and cultural evolution.[4] That process has produced in us a propensity toward altruism as a major mechanism to support the survival of the tribe/community/group. Our prism through which to consider this concept is the discipline of ethics. The effect of acknowledging and helping other humans ensures better survival of the group. Compounding this, cultures often seek to reward individuals who engage in the socially useful activity.

Therefore, it is a product of evolution that we humans will be more supportive of the group that we live in rather than other groups. Social biology suggests that discrimination between humans by humans is what has allowed us to evolve into what we are today (see the postscript to chapter 3). Discrimination between humans has been tempered over time as our intellect evolved to a point at which humans could consider the question, Is the discrimination truly important—does the sex or skin color of a human support continuing the discrimination? Definitely not. What about mental or physical abilities? Perhaps yes. Should anyone with the desire to attend law school be admitted? Almost all law schools discriminate on some basis. Different human cultures answer that question of acceptability of discrimination differently. But even in the United States, which seeks a heartfelt national policy of nondiscrimination, we have different communities of which we are a part. The biological urge to discriminate and the intellectual belief that we should not discriminate is a tension within the human mind that is unavoidable and most likely will always be present.

If we humans inherently discriminate and form communities, then there are two key questions within the focus of this book. First, what defines a community? Some are defined by genes; and others, by geography. Second, just who is within the community? Is it possible that some animals are in some of our groups and that therefore we need to be supportive of and respectful of animals as well as humans? This book supports the expansion of human groups to include animals. The animals are physically present already; the issue is whether they can be given the status of community membership rather than being just a community resource. It is the combination of heart and mind that will provide the answer for each individual human. The correctness of the obligations to others within the group depends upon the nature of the group. There are no universal answers to the simple question, How should I treat non-human animals?

The Selfish Center

It can't be helped,
We are born
Within
Our Selfish Center.

Can we,
Will we,
Push away?
Moving outward.

Join with,
Other
Selfish Centers?

Creating a Center
Apart from
Any
One.

TWO NEW CONCEPTS

Ethical Weight

While it may be the case that many readers of this book are willing to acknowledge the existence of a duty toward the well-being of animals, there is always the more difficult question, How much duty? And, how does my duty to animals relate to my duty to other humans? Since these are personal judgments, there are no firm answers. The questions place everyone on a slippery slope. The following is a context in which to consider the complex issues of duty to others. The extent of ethical obligations, in part, can be considered as a force of nature, much like the pull of gravity; the closer the relationships, the greater the feeling of weight. The level of attraction and, therefore, the weight of the duty is proportional to the importance of community that the two humans (or the human and the animal) share.

Again, this is a matter of personal ethics; the sorting of the importance of the different communities is personal. Communities are important to a particular person based upon that person's life experiences, mental capacity, and personality. The most important community to many individuals is that of family, with its strong degree of genetic relationship and emotional bonds of love. The least important shared community is that of simply being a human, each unknown and unrelated to the other, perhaps half a world away. Obviously, there is considerable room for a diverse set of weights reflecting the many different communities of which each human is a part. The value of each community is personal to the individual and may well change significantly over time. This approach accepts the reality that our ethical duties to humans are not equal but are context dependent. One objective measure of each individual's judgment in this matter can be obtained by considering which organizations and individuals a person supports with time and money. A sense of ethical duty is the motivation for such support, but seldom does a person give equal amounts of time or money to all the groups or people toward which they feel a duty. Of course, this book urges that animals are also owed ethical duties based upon the threshold concept of them being ethical subjects. Again, ethical weight can help sort the extent and nature of the duty.

While it is expected that many different outcomes exist for ethical duties, legal duties are different. If you are within a country, you do not have the ability to decline the laws of the country, even if you disagree with them. It takes an aggregate of personal ethics to adopt a prohibiting law. For example, it is considered by many to be unethical to use ten-year-olds to make commercial products in a factory. If a child-labor law is adopted, it is binding on all who live in that political jurisdiction, regardless of personal ethics. The political state of which we are a citizen is perhaps one of the most important communities that a human is part of, because the laws of the state will supersede personal ethical positions in a number of animal-related contexts. Additionally, we delegate to the state most of our ethical duties that we have to fellow citizens, for example, support of the elderly by Social Security payments. In the absence of a law, it is a personal, ethical decision (or, if not of an individual, then that of a corporate board of directors or a religious organization) about whether or not to use young children within the commercial production context.

After a consideration of human communities and the more important animal/human communities, the concept of ethical weight will be touched upon again.

Civitist

A civitist is someone who actively engages in the creation of positive communities, like perhaps digging a frog pond or planting milkweed as a rest stop for butterflies, or building a new habitat for quail. Thus the concept of community is critical to the task of deciding not only upon ethical principles for action or inaction within a community but also on what communities may need to be created and supported.

INTRODUCTION TO COMMUNITIES

One proposal of this book is the need to create positive ethical obligations upon humans for the creation of better and stronger positive communities between humans, and between humans and animals. This is particularly critical for wildlife, which needs more than the existing legal restraints to prevent unnecessary harm. We humans need to recognize an affirmative duty to create the physical spaces and conditions for vibrant ecological communities. Those who adopt this ethical duty go beyond being an environmentalist who seeks to do no harm to existing ecosystems. Rather, a civitist accepts the affirmative responsibility for the creation and maintenance of more positive communities and, in particular, physical communities for wildlife to inhabit and proliferate.

THE FROG POND

On our farm in Michigan, my wife and I have intentionally created a place of death, of pain, and of life. This is a small effort to carry out my affirmative ethical duty to support other life. We had a hole dug—perhaps fifteen feet across and four feet deep at the center—then we added some water, plants, and six goldfish from the local grocery store. We stirred and waited a few years. Now we have a thriving and complex ecosystem. A number of species of frogs have arrived, two small turtles for one summer, and a number of native plants. I take pride in my pond's existence and find great pleasure in contemplating it, as it passes through the four seasons of the year. The goldfish have moved through a number of generations, but none of the original six lived past the Black Day of the Blue Heron. There has been life and death within and above the waters. Spring evenings hear the croaking of the frogs seeking to find a mate. But we have also heard a frog scream as he was eaten by a snake. Each summer, a dragonfly arrives to take charge of the air over the pond. Snails seek to consume the detritus of death. But all users of the frog pond are not wild; the chickens are occasional visitors to drink the water, and even a cat or dog has been known to take a sip.

Although I do not make individual decisions about the animals in the pond, it is still an ecosystem requiring management. Some plants would take over the entire pond if given a chance; too much organic material would choke the pond if left alone. (The happiest river birch in Michigan, planted by us, lives on the edge of this pond and now reaches fifty feet in the air.) However, the pond would dry up in a few weeks if I did not keep a continuous small stream of water flowing into it. I have created and managed a place for the diversity of life to discover and occupy, and nature has done so very well, I rejoice in its magic and complexity.

For visitors, especially children, it is the introduction to a farm full of life, a farm that is a space for both nature's diversity and our own interests. It is a space to share the ecosystem of pasture with nature and domestic animals; there is a sense of harmony and balance. To stand in our pasture with grasses and alfalfa up to our waist, is to stand in ecological riches that are entirely apart from the abstraction of human money.

Figure 5.1.

The pond is reflective of several of the overlapping communities that one simple human shares with an assortment of individual animals: a community with wildlife, a community with commercial domestic animals, and a community with companion animals. My ethical obligation differs depending on the shared community even if we exist on the same farm.

Time has passed since I first drafted the above, and while the modest frog pond continues to exist, we have more recently had the opportunity to bring into being a much larger pond toward the back of our property. So our creative community-building venture continues on a much larger scale.

Figure 5.2.

CHAPTER 6

HUMAN COMMUNITIES

Communities

We are born into them,
We grow,
We learn,
We propagate,
Within our differing communities.

We travel between them,
We create them,
We might destroy them.

Communities
Define us,
Constrain us,
Comfort and distress us.

Fulfillment is in
Supporting, building,
Shaping,
Your communities.

Death will come,
For you and I,
But our communities,
Continue,
Marching forward,
As waves crossing the sea.

What is the definition of a community: a unified body of individuals; a group of people with common interests, usually living in a particular area; a group of people with a common characteristic, or common policy, or common history?

Possible communities include:

Families:
By blood and by marriage
Ethnic background

Economic activity:
Work communities
Consumer communities

Spiritual interest:
Religious communities

Shared experience:
University attendance
Boy Scouts or Girl Scouts
Military service / soldiers from a war
Visitors to Yellowstone National Park
University community

Shared interests:
Garden club
Poetry reading
Stamp collecting
Cancer survivor
Internet groups

Physical location:
Neighborhood
Hometown
State or national residence

Global:
> The community of humans
> The community of members of nature in its entirety

Ecological:
> Mountains of Colorado
> Great Lakes
> Key West

Historically, human communities have had a very strong geographic component. The family, job, religious group, friends, and social groups were all in the same location. Knowledge and awareness of "others" might extend only a hundred miles or so. Today the Internet and transmission of information and pictures has greatly extended the possibility of creating communities with others not in one's geographic area. But it is harder to sort out the nature of ethical duties toward individuals one has never met in person but only know on Facebook or interact with on Skype. For animals, they remain primarily a community defined with geographic boundaries. This idea will be developed in the next chapter.

How many communities are you a part of? The human need for group membership is as fundamental to our nature as is the desire to reproduce, both being key elements for our evolutionary success. Everyone's list of his or her personal communities is long and complex. Who is important to you, and why are they important? To what or whom do you give time and money? These questions will reveal your important communities. We do not view our ethical duties toward individuals in different communities as the same. That I share a work space with someone or an interest in stamp collecting with another does not suggest I have a duty to help by loaning this other person my car whenever he or she might need it. But for some family members, perhaps I should. I am willing to share the cost of a new road at my local government level, but not for an area in Brazil. Since this is a rather self-evident reality, I will not dwell upon it here.

Don't forget that even while different communities make different demands upon you, your judgment about how much you respect specific individuals at particular moments in time will play a role in your ethical decisions. At work, some individuals will be more respected than others, allowing a high ethical obligation within that community. But when a community is composed of individuals whom you do not know personally, it is difficult for you to respect the individual, but you may still respect for the group, which will give rise to certain types of general duties and actions.

It will be useful, however, to pursue this idea of relative duty into the area of law for a moment. The present culture of the United States is dominated by the concept of equality and inclusion, as evidenced by the common phrase "we are all equal in the eyes of the law." Our Declaration of Independence begins with a sweeping ethical statement:

> We hold these truths to be self-evident, that all men are created equal, that they are endowed by their Creator with certain unalienable Rights, which among these are Life, Liberty and the pursuit of Happiness.

Of course, even when adopted by our white male Founders, this statement was not really true, but it has become the aspirational goal for our legal system and culture generally, and many federal and state laws have been passed to ensure equal treatment for all humans. While this concept is indeed a foundational principle of law within the United States, there are significant boundaries on the concept of equality. The law has many categories that allow for unequal treatment of humans. For example, if you have been criminally convicted of a felony act, you do not have equal rights in civil participation, with limited voting rights or the right to own a gun. If you are a sex offender, you do not have equal rights of privacy. You must call in to your parole officer or be available to the local police at all times. Furthermore, your address is always made public: anyone with access to the Internet can find out where you live. For instance, the equal protection guaranteed by the Fourteenth Amendment to the US Consti-

ow,
ling

ities
posi-
legal
not
er in
hical
ts of
livid-
vern-
gram
these
legal
e and
gh the

treat
use of
ngage-
camera
ry that
action
ommu-
rs. The
action.
is pos-
als dif-
s based
eatment
, that is,

es a citizen as all persons born in the United States or
ng become a citizen, clearly applies only to citizens of
ot to all human beings who happen to be within the
United States.

our law, the most important community is that com-
essing full US citizenship. These individuals receive
f being within the community. But others, like those
e a member of this political community, may well
t, if not impossible. Our community is not willing
on the Earth to decide for himself that he wants to
the United States. Indeed, sometimes our law draws
out who is allowed in and who is not. A marvelous
rimination is evidenced by the treatment of people
Cuba to come to the United States, for many years.
a and are found in our territorial waters by US gov-
are summarily removed from the United States.
n our system, no provision for due process of law.
e from Cuba but manage to arrive and walk upon
special status under immigration law and consider-
again, if you walk across the Mexican border into
u are deemed an illegal immigrant who has only
procedural rights. If you are a prisoner of the US
held outside the United States (for example, in the
ntion camp), you do not have the same legal rights
ere or the rights of a foreign person visiting within

an argument for or against any of these policies,
t legal rights are dependent on the community of
rson belongs. The 2013–2014 debate in the US
ration bill suggested widely different ethical views
lowed within our political community and eligible
ns of the constitution and the benefits of our insti-

tutions and programs. This issue is not going away any time soo
in 2018, Congress is continuing to try to work something out re
immigration and the legal status of persons residing in the countr

Even when individuals are within a political community, th
imposed by the law can differ. Consider when a person might hav
tive legal duty of care toward another human. I have an ethical a
duty to care for my daughter until she is able to care for herself.
have a legal duty to provide care to my neighbor, let alone a str
another town. However, many people have voluntarily adopted a
view that includes a duty of care for other people, and throug
charity, they help others. This ethical duty is held by enough
uals that it is also reflected in public policy, being one basis for
ment programs such as the Supplemental Nutrition Assistance
(SNAP), our food stamp program for those in need. But of cou
programs are often limited only to US citizens and those hav
status in our country. This is because the commitment to pro
pay for services comes out of our shared political community thr
taxes citizens pay.

While on some abstract level we might have a moral duty
all humans with equal concern, it is impossible to do so, both b
limited resources and because we lack an emotional capacity for
ment with unseen people around the world. It is only when th
brings before us the faces of starving children from another cou
our emotions awaken, and upon this response social and politic
can be built. The pictures bring the otherwise unseen into our
nity, at least visually, making it harder to ignore the needs of ot
logic of human equality is always present, but emotion motivate

Given that our legal system does not treat all people equally,
sible to understand how the legal system also treats groups of an
ferently. While some humans seek to differentiate animal spec
upon biological characteristics, it is more useful to adjust legal t
according to the nature of the animals' relationship with humar

which community they share with humans. Understanding the existence of different animal/human communities is critical to understanding the different ethical obligations that might arise or how the legal system might insist upon different levels of care and concern.

> Who is part of your "give a hug to" community? Any animals? Why, why not?

CHAPTER 7

HUMAN COMMUNITIES WITH ANIMALS

The list of possible human communities is almost without end; and while many are not populated with animals, some very important ones are. Our communities with animals tend to be focused by physical location: on the farm, in the forest, in the laboratory, or in the home. The following identifies some of the most important communities; others certainly exist. These communities will provide ample opportunity for the application of the ethical concept of respectful use. Again, the threshold question will be, Which animals are or should be considered ethical subjects, rather than mere personal property, within a particular community?

We are a sight-driven species (although not all individual humans have the capacity for sight, of course). What is important to us is usually within our viewing, or direct contact. It is in our nature to care about that which we can see or experience firsthand. Our motivations for ethical obligations are primarily driven by those we see, those we know, and those with whom we interact. In the online world of today, we can see much more than we used to see. But, you might say, what about all the others we don't see; don't we have a duty to them as well? What duty we may have to them is very light, but that is acceptable because if each human dealt ethically with those around him or her, then our concerns about those out of our sight would be considerably allayed. Everyone should be within the sight of someone.

This problem of unseen others is even more difficult when the ethical subjects are animals. In the communities with animals set out below, some animals are not seen by any humans, others are seen by humans lacking the capacity to do anything for the animal, and still others are seen daily by some human with the capacity to help or harm the animal.

As we proceed through the following communities, there is one significant factor that helps predict the level of risk that an animal will be treated disrespectfully. Does the owner of the animal share a physical space with the animal such that the owner is able to literally "see" the animal as an individual, to see the eyes of the animal looking back at him or her? For us humans, eye contact can create bonds of awareness and respect. When animals have no eye contact with humans, there is a higher risk of disrespectful use and thus a greater need for external intervention, including prohibitive and protective laws.

THE COMMUNITY OF COMPANIONS (OF FAMILY)

On the whole, animals with which people have the closest personal relationships can be classified as pets or companions. These animals are easily identified because they have been given names and usually live with people. Horses and other large animals that are not brought into the physical space of the home may be companions nevertheless, but the line is more difficult to discern. The other critical identifier of a companion animal is that there is at least one human within the family who has a strong emotional attachment to the animal, which is usually reciprocated. Millions of people have formed such attachments with animals, populating the animal-companion community with millions of animals. But there is the goldfish-in-the-tank issue. Does mere physical presence make it part of the community of the family? In some cases, fish are merely moving decorations within a home, not unlike a light display or a lava lamp. While it is possible for a human to have an attachment to a goldfish, it is doubtful that the emotional attachment is reciprocated. For the purposes of this discussion, the focus is on mammals as companions; lizards and fish can be the consideration of another day. (I suspect that many would claim that lizards, snakes, and such similar creatures do bond with their humans.)

It is stating the obvious that companion animals are treated differently than cows in the field or eagles in the sky. They are treated differently not because of inherent moral worth or legal requirements, but because they are not found existing within the important community of the family. Here people show friendship and individual care for animals, a relationship usually considered a social good for the human and the animal. (Some people become hoarders of animals under the cover of caring about companion animals, but hoarders do not understand that they often inflict harm upon the animals under their control.) A fair presumption is that if an animal is sharing a living space with a human family, then he or she is a companion animal. But this can be rebutted in individual sets of circumstances. What about a service animal that helps a handicapped individual recognize the onset of a seizure, or one that provides sound or sight assistance for a specific human? They are normally within the living space of the human family, and it might be expected that a service animal and the human have an emotional attachment, but if they do not, then the service animal will be in the broader category of working animals.

The initial dog that we met, Rover, was in the home of Homer, and therefore he was presumed to be a companion animal. When a family makes a visit to the zoo, they see many animals, but none of them would be considered a companion animal, since they are not admitted into the family. How about hunting dogs kept in kennels in the backyard or guard dogs chained to trees in the front yard? These animals perform services for humans but are not, for the most part, thought to be within a specific family community. Because they have not been admitted into the home, they do not have a presumption of companionship. However, they could still qualify as a member of the companion community with the showing of an emotional attachment and personal concern by some member of the family. Otherwise, they also will fall into the category of working animals, which will be discussed below.

COMMUNITY WITH WORKING ANIMALS

This community contains many different activities, and it is a bit of a catchall category for domestic animals. If an animal/human relationship does not fit in any of the other categories, then the animal should go here. Humans have interacted with animals with many different motives, including economic profit, performance of labor, and entertainment. Unlike the next category, food animals within industrial facilities, the animals in this category do not have to die to perform their human-desired function. The animals in the zoo, or in a circus, or show animals that are not companions, and most domestic horses are all part of this community. If a hunting or show dog is not a companion, then he will fit in here. While it is possible that some of these animals will have human caregivers that form an emotional connection with the animal, it is usually not by the owner of the animal. When ownership is by a corporation, it is not possible for the creation of an emotional attachment between the owner and the individual animal; it is well understood that corporations as such are entities without he capacity for human feeling or emotion. Thus, the groom of a racehorse may have a deep affection for a horse in her care, but that human does not have control over the key decisions about the well-being of the horse: whether or not to race, to breed, to give drugs, and to live.

Dolphins at aquariums, dogs caged for commercial breeding, animals bred for research purposes, and big cats held by private individuals in backyard cages are all examples of the working-animal category. What constitutes respectful use of these animals can sometimes be difficult to judge. If they have been captured in the wild, then those animals are at more risk of disrespectful use, because they have been removed from their natural habitat.

Even wild animals can become part of this community when captured to become part of the world of human entertainment. For example, consider the life of Keiko the orca whale, who became a celebrity in the *Free Willy* movies. In 1993, the first of three movies featuring Keiko was released by Warner Brothers. The film is about a boy who befriends a whale, Willy. The whale was a wild animal that came within the community of humans and was given a name. He bridged the gulf between anonymous wildlife and part of our entertainment community. Keiko was not only a pet to some individual humans who cared for him but also part of our pop culture. After his movie years, there was great debate about what was in his best interest—to stay in the company of humans or to be released back into the wild. A long story followed, but ultimately millions of dollars were spent trying to teach him to survive again in his natural environment. However, when he was released into the open ocean, he did not bond with fellow whales. Instead, he showed a preference for the company of humans. He lived his final retirement years in a Norwegian fjord, voluntarily interacting with the tourists who sought him out, and he was fed every day by his human support group. While perhaps a few people would have been willing to kill him as just another whale, most people would have morally rejected the killing and eating of Keiko, since he was not really wildlife but was within the human community as an individual, even if not a pet.[1] He was part of a one-person retirement community for whales.

COMMUNITY WITH LOCAL WILDLIFE

Before the first dogs or cats joined human families as companions, humans shared their local space with wildlife. Indeed, the presence of local wildlife was often critical to the survival of the families. These were the animals living alongside humans, sharing the same space. The wild animals at the zoo are not part of this community, regardless of the number of humans who see them in their cages. Also, a rabbit born in the wild but caught and put in a cage in the backyard is no longer a part of the local wildlife community.

This community is defined by a "not" rather than an "is." A member of the local wildlife community is not the property of people or corporations and is not under human dominion and control. Ever since the time of the Romans, legal systems have dealt with the distinction between wild and domestic animals by creating rules for the legal transformation of wild animals into human personal property.[2] In theory at least, wildlife lead an independent life, perhaps in parallel with humans. But a human's view of wildlife is strongly influenced by the cultural context in which the person lives. Wildlife may be considered a source of dinner; a source of income; a source of entertainment; or simply part of a wilderness experience, not to be killed or captured. We in the United States seldom rely on wildlife for daily subsistence or for economic return, unlike the frontier days, when wildlife meat and pelts could be sold as commodities. And that cultural context shapes our ethical relationship and rules of law dealing with this category of animal. But for all cases of local wildlife, there is an ecosystem shared by both. For a farmer in rural areas, this can be a robust relationship with daily interactions with many species of animals. The interactions can be positive or negative, as when the wild raccoon eats the newly laid free-range chicken eggs. In a city, it is a more modest community, but one that exists nevertheless (and, yes, the rats and pigeons are part of that local wildlife community).

On my farm, there is an extensive local wildlife community. The frogs in my pond; the deer and snakes in my field; and the dozens of bird species, at our feeders or not, are all local wildlife sharing the same ecosystem. There is an enhanced duty to local wildlife because of the physical proximity of the animals; this duty is not going to be due to wildlife in the next category of animals, the community of global wildlife.[3]

Think about It

I am sitting at the kitchen table in my parent's home in Florida, reading the local paper. The headlines suggest the dilemma that humans face in defining the nature of their community with wild animals. "New Jersey's Bear Hunt Ends; 328 Confirmed Dead." The state of New Jersey had just allowed the first bear hunt in thirty-three years. They were hoping to kill upward of 500 of the 3,200 bears in the state to stop the "rising tide of complaints" about the bears in suburban areas. The other headline, on the next page, reads: "Woman Raises, Releases Orphaned Bears." The story tells us that for more than eighteen years, a woman had cared for and released thirty-five bear cubs and was presently working with four more.[4]

In this latter case, we can see that some individual animals cross the lines between communities. What can I say? Is this woman's life's work foolish or noble?

Sometimes it is the animal that chooses to cross over from one community to another.

The Dog and the Wolf
Shall Not Lie Down Together

The following is an e-mail my wife and I received because we are part of the ISBONA (Icelandic Sheep Breeders) Community; it is reproduced here with permission.

To: ISBONA List serve
From: Yeomen Farm, Canada
Date: Oct. 20, 2004
Subject: GOLSA

My dear old pet Golsa is no more. She was killed this morning by wolves. I let all the ewes out shortly after 9 this morning and sometime after that all the ewes came home. I was busy shearing so I had not followed them out to the pasture as usual. Around 10:30 we were finished and I decided to go out on the pasture for exercise. I came over the hill and at the bottom, 200 feet away was Athena, our guardian dog standing over a creature that I thought was a dog that one of the people in the village had lost a few days ago. As soon as Athena looked up, waving her tail at me, the "dog" took off and I saw it was an eastern red wolf. Athena took after it. I ran home yelling at Ray to come out and both of us went down to the pasture. I was a bit ahead and then I saw a grayish hump. It was Golsa. Torn apart, but with head intact. I thought I was past emotional reactions over killed sheep—but I am not.

We looked for the wolf in the pasture Athena had chased it into but did not find it. However, I saw a wolf in another pasture further away. We went there but it was gone too. While we were having lunch I looked out of a window where I could see Golsa's remains and the wolf was back. We tried to get there without being seen, but the wolf took off. Now Ray is stalking the wolf, waiting for it to come back.

Many of you do have Golsa in your sheep's pedigree. She was STS 37Z-416054—a remarkable sheep and one of my special ones. You will probably read more about her in our Newsletter, when I will be feeling a bit better.

Stefania
Icelandic sheep since 1985

The expectation of Stefania was that the dog would guard the sheep from the harm and death caused by wild predators such as the wolf she saw. And yet, she saw them together. The members of these two different communities seemed to be mingling, standing together over the carcass of Golsa. (She was one of the first ewes of the Icelandic breed in North America, and indeed one of our sheep does have her as an ancestor.) A subsequent e-mail from Stefania made this situation even more complex when she reported seeing the wolf and the previously spayed guard dog coming out of the edge of the woods together. Has the dog changed the community with which she identifies? Some stories will never be fully known. Stefania's experience detailed above is not an unusual blending of pet animals, traditional farm animals, and local wildlife.

COMMUNITY WITH GLOBAL WILDLIFE

We do not see whales on a daily basis, so we cannot consider them local wildlife. Similarly, the great apes of the wild, the elephants of Africa, and penguins of the Antarctic are far removed from our daily lives. This community of global wildlife encompasses all wildlife that is not part of the community with local wildlife as experienced by each individual. To a local landowner, an eagle may be a member of local wildlife, since the bird uses the lake on her land; to me, the eagle is unseen and therefore one of thousands in the global wildlife community. Your link to any one individual animal across the world is very thin, but, in the aggregate of millions of animals in the global wildlife community, the link has a cumulative weight supporting a duty toward the unseen. This community is tied together with two threads. First is the linkage of shared genetic heritage. While we are most like other humans around the world, we share a DNA heritage with all mammals, and, going further and further back in time, with all animals. It is perhaps the ultimate in diluted family relationships. But if aliens were ever to arrive from a distant galaxy, we humans would not have that DNA linkage with the aliens, even though they would presumably be living beings. (This suggests an even-larger community: that of all living beings of the universe—but I'm not going to push that thought until they reveal themselves more fully or we manage to find them.)

Perhaps more important than the genetic link with wildlife is the fact that we share our present lives through the larger ecosystems we cohabit. A mere two hundred years ago, when the global human population was only one billion versus the seven billion of today and ten billion of the future, human cohabitation was not threatening to the global wildlife, because human activity did not seem capable of impacting the ecosystems or the wildlife therein on a global basis. Today, however, it is clear that humans do impact whole ecosystems and the wildlife therein, and, therefore, humans must confront the consequences of their choices in an ethical context.

The first means by which ecosystems are impacted is by the destruction or transformation of land at the local level around the world by individual humans and the businesses they create. There are two different types of human impact on local lands and wildlife. First, the increasing number of humans around the world requires the consumption and transformation of the places they live. The energy, food production, housing, and transportation necessary to support increasing numbers of humans can significantly alter, if not destroy, local ecosystems. The consequences to the environment, our shared ecosystem, of having another human child born seems so modest that it almost never is a factor in a couple's decision to have a child, but in the aggregate the consequences on a global scale are considerable. Future additional billions of humans are a great threat to an already-fragile Earth.

The second human factor resulting in ecosystem destruction arises out of increasing monetary wealth in a globally traded world. As millions of humans reach the position of middle class and the number of millionaires climbs ever higher, consuming an increasing amount of goods from around the world becomes highly likely. When this happens, there is a disconnection between what is seen by the consumer (the product) and what was not seen by the consumer (the environmental consequences of the manufacture of that product). For example, what are the consequences to the oceans of the world when ten million sharks are killed so that shark-fin soup can be served as a marker of wealth in the Far East? Likewise, what if someone buys a jar of palm oil at the local store? Does he know where it came from, how much wildlife was killed or displaced, and how much habitat was lost in the creation of the palm-oil plantations? In Indonesia, upward of four million hectares (twelve million acres) of wildlife habitat has been destroyed for the creation of palm-oil plantations.[5] We consumers in the West do not see the wildlife killed or displaced by the clearing of land. There is no pile of bodies to give witness to the destruction; they simply disappear. We can only imagine the wildlife that might have lived on the land in the past (see chapter 13, "We Are the Gods of Old").

While every human individually is part of a local wildlife community, they together are also part of the global community of wildlife that comprises all the wildlife that is not part of their local community. The ethical discussion about this community will not be about a duty to individual animals, as it might be for a companion animal, but rather for the aggregate of millions of unseen animals. We share Earth with ethical subjects we do not know, tied together by our global ecological systems. What ought to be our obligations toward them?

COMMUNITY WITH INDUSTRIAL AGRICULTURAL ANIMALS VERSUS HISTORICAL AGRICULTURAL ANIMALS

Beyond the daily interface with companion animals, the most common exposure humans have to animals is the consumption of their bodies for human food: the agricultural food animal. These animals differ from those in the working-animal community because the animal's flesh or product—meat, poultry, eggs, or milk—is sold directly to the consumer. The purpose of this ownership has a primary motivation of economic profit; perhaps it is the sole purpose of ownership. This is the community that has the highest risk of disconnect between the human owners and the individual animals, thus possessing the highest risk of disrespectful use. These animals (chickens, hogs, feedlot cattle, and others) are not seen every day by someone inherently concerned with their welfare. Most contacts are by unskilled, uninterested workers who do not seek any connection with the animals. For example, consider the building that has no windows but twenty thousand egg-laying chickens, with automatic water and feeders, and automatic egg collectors. What are the odds that anyone ever looks at the individual beings stuffed five or six to a cage?[6] (The brutal conditions faced by some industrial animals will not be detailed in this book. Numerous books and websites exist to explain and show the grisly details. I am not a dispassionate observer of these conditions, but I choose not to dwell on them here.)

Personal connections may exist on many small, family farms, but to say that a facility is owned by a family does not mean it can be removed from the industrial-agriculture category. On the other hand, the presumption of disrespectful use by a large or corporate facility does not mean it is impossible for respectful use of agricultural animals, since the owners can intentionally set into place rules about the conditions of the animals' lives that move toward the judgment of respectful use.

Respectful use is much more likely when the animals are seen by their owner(s). On family farms, historically, ownership and direct oversight of daily care were combined in the same person or family. A person had to like the company of animals to spend his or her life raising and working with them. Over the past thousands of years, family farms have represented the vast majority of human-animal relationships. They are the sheep cared for by the shepherds of the Bible. They are the chicks and cows on Old MacDonald's farm. They are the animals cared for by their owners, even if the owners use them to their advantage. The thirty pigs in a fenced field or barnyard, even though not named by the family, are cared for each day by someone of the family; the quality of life and health are easily tracked by those with the responsibility to care for the animals.

Disrespectful use is much more likely when the animals are not seen by those with the power to shape the lives of the animals. Our ethical and legal goals should be to eliminate the unseen animals and support and encourage communities in which agricultural animals are seen animals.

And, of course, on the other side, just because a human has only a few animals to deal with and sees them on a regular basis does not mean that they will be treated respectfully in a specific case. This is when the law needs to step forward and make demands of minimum care.

Where the risk of disrespect is high, the animals will be denoted as industrial agricultural animals. Where the risk is low, the animals will be denoted as historical agricultural animals. The term "historical" is meant to refer to the period before 1940, when almost all farming was organic and small-scale. Not that a replication of exact historical conditions is sought or suggested by this reference. But best outcomes for today will arise when the scale that can be humane is combined with the scientific information and technologies of today. The term "historic" rather than "traditional" was used as a descriptor of this community because some of the industrial practices have been in place for forty or more years, and it is not clear how long something has to continue before it is considered traditional.

THE COMMUNITY OF OUR KNOWLEDGE SEEKERS OF SELF AND SOCIETY

This is a set of animals that are apart from working animals generally because the motivation for their use is the obtaining of information or knowledge by those who own the animals. However, this category must be considered to possess two subparts: those activities that seek to expand the knowledge of science and those that expand only the knowledge of particular individuals. The latter arises in the areas of education and testing where science gains no new information but only the individual who is engaging in the action does. Science uses large numbers of animals in seeking the cure for cancer. Some cosmetic companies also use live animals to test the safety of commercial products, but this does not produce new information important to science. Since most people would assign different values to these two activities, they will be treated separately when determining a judgment about their ethical use.

It is assumed by most observers that millions of mice are used each year in research, but since there is no legal duty or legal requirement to report the number of mice or rats used in research, the actual number is not known. Other mammals such as dogs, cats, primates, and rabbits are also used and counted. (In 2016, US institutions reported using 71,188 primates [the vast majority are monkeys], 60,979 dogs, and 139,391 rabbits in scientific research involving pain.[7])

NEGATIVE COMMUNITIES

The community of humans seeking to create entertainment and profit by the fighting of dogs or other animals is a longstanding outlawed community. While not yet dealing with judgments about respectful use, this is a fairly clear example, at least in the United States, of a community that has been judged by a majority of citizens as disrespectful, unhealthy, and unacceptably inflicting pain and suffering. As a result of this judgment, I will categorize dogfighting and other forms of animal fighting as a negative community. This ethical judgment is so strong that under many state and federal laws it is a felony to be a dogfighter or cockfighter. It is usually a crime to even seek to join the community by attending a dogfight or a cockfight.

Another repulsive community that a few humans have created with animals involves the death of a small animal in a human sexual context. With the internet has come awareness that some humans are recording and distributing "crush videos." (Crush videos are defined as fetish videos in which small animals are taunted, tortured, and then crushed to death under the feet of provocatively dressed women.) This is wrong at so many levels that such activity, and the recording and distribution of such videos, quickly became illegal at the national level.[8]

As will be shown, some communities created by humans will be made illegal, as the above examples show, while others will have to be regulated to assure that they are ethically acceptable. The community of commercial blood bullfighting, in which the bull is killed as a climax to the event, is representative of one activity perceived as both positive and negative in cultures in countries such as Spain and Mexico.

THE COMMUNITY OF GENETIC CREATION

In all of the above categories, it has been assumed that the animals in question came to life through natural birth, with perhaps a little help by humans motivated to engage in selective breeding for traits useful to humans. But there is now a new category of animal that is expected to increase considerably in the future. These animals may or may not be commercial, be found in the wild, or have personal names. The defining factor is that they result from genetic manipulation beyond that of historical selective breeding. The first step down this path was represented by the cloning of Dolly the sheep in 1996. Today it is possible to clone a pet.[9] The next step was when the DNA from different species were mixed to create a new animal. For example, the GloFish carries mixed genes from different species.[10] Human genes may be mixed with the genes of chickens, pigs, and sheep to produce an assortment of products.[11] Perhaps in the future this community will include chickens that have no feelings and can be kept in the dark to save a little money, or pigs that carry human genes in order to provide beneficial hormones. This community differs from the others because we are not just the keepers of these animals but their creators. Perhaps in time this category will dissipate into the other four, but for now, with the genetic processes so new and so risky, and with the field so wide open, they deserve special consideration. Ethically speaking, the risk is the experiment that doesn't work, the one that results in creatures that may be malformed and die or be in pain.

An Occasional Very Short (Fictional) Story

What if, by some biotechnical means, changing genes resulted in enhancing the intellect of animals? What if they could demand their rights? What then?

The Uplifting

It seemed reasonable enough at the time, but then it always does. The intelligence-enhancing drug Genioxtum had been available for humans for about a year outside the United States.

The drug worked by resetting the timer on the genes in the brain that created the neural network during the first two years of brain growth in humans. Many millions of potential neuron cells are created in the brain during that time, but many never become integrated into the neural net and die off. The drug allowed the genes to again create a surplus of neuron cells. The treatment would not have any effect unless the individual was placed in an enriched sensory environment full of new information, requiring the brain to store, sort, and organize the new materials—then the new cells would create new, stronger networks of information. The increase in intelligence was the result not of the new information per se but arose because 10 percent of the cells formed a bigger, more robust network that managed the new information, enhancing the ability to see patterns in the information. Intelligence is a function not of information storage but of the structure of neurons created to do pattern identification within the information, resulting in an understanding of that information.

Someone was curious about what would happen if Genioxtum were to be administered to a dog. Of course, because the neuron network of a dog is fundamentally like that of humans, it was just as effective. The key to having the drug work was finding the super-enrichment environment that would set up the enhanced neuron-network in the brain. For the dogs researchers decided on exposing them to classical music and the SS–HDTV (smell and sound enhanced) for three two-hour segments each day. The dogs had been on the drug for about three weeks when a few small changes were noticed. The investigators swore that they saw the animals smile at mirror images of themselves. Second, the animals started engaging in devious but cooperative behavior in order to get their handlers to give them more food. About six weeks into the experiment, the investigators knew something had happened when the dogs appeared to be bored watching cartoons and seemed to pay attention to baseball games. There was even one particular dog that showed a preference for the talking heads of the O channel (Opinions Only, 24/7).

The investigators never did figure out how the animals contacted the attorneys who filed the petition for their release from the lab as enhanced animals capable of self-sufficiency and, therefore, deserving of liberty from human control. Of course, with attorneys always filing crazy things, the court and world were not impressed until the dogs were shown to score in the range of 90 to108 on the standardized IQ test. (The Chihuahua scored only a 60, but no one considered him part of the enhancement program, since he was the pet of a lab technician who had been slipped a few pills.)

> Will human-enhanced intelligence
> in animals change our ethical duties
> toward them?

CHAPTER 8

WE ALL HAVE INTERESTS

IF SOMETHING IS ALIVE, IT HAS INTERESTS

The word "interests," as in the interests of humans or dogs, is an important concept because the process of deciding ethical conduct toward others will necessarily require the balancing of often-conflicting interests. What are the interests of the ethical actor (you) and the ethical subject (the animal)? Take, for example, that you have the need to get to work on time, but your companion animal has an interest in play or in eating breakfast. What is the ethically correct outcome? It is unclear because the term "interest" is a bit too loose to help sort the important from the trivial. For purposes of this discussion, the concept is split into two major categories.

The first category of interests is designated as "biologically provided self-interests." These are interests that arise out of the evolution of our DNA. Some are obvious: the need for oxygen so cells can create energy, a diet of a variety of foods so different cells can perform their function, clothes to protect our bodies from negative external factors, and to be a part of a community (hopefully a positive community).

A second type of interest is at least one step removed from biological interests and can be referred to as "experience interests." These are the desires of individuals that arise out of the life experience of an individual. Homer, the dog owner we met earlier in the book, along with all other humans, has an interest in the consumption of food to retain health and life. Homer, and not all other humans, has found a focus for this interest in the consumption of cherry pies. While all humans have a genetically provided interest in the seeking out of sugar, not all humans have an interest in cherry pies. While cherry pies are a source of sugar, such pies, per se, are not required for the sustaining of life. The preference or interest in cherry pie is most likely a result of childhood positive experiences. This interest itself usually has no ethical consequence even though it might impact the waistline of Homer. However, a professor of logic might suggest: if he eats too many cherry pies, then he will become a diabetic or have a heart attack and die young, thus not fulfilling his ethical duty to provide a full life of support and comfort to his wife and children. But I will ignore that chain of thought.

We will need to sort, to give weight to, a wide variety of interests in ethical decision-making. We will also need to sort those interests that are so important as to justify the adoption of laws to control human conduct from inappropriate interference (freedom from torture, for example). One premise of this discussion is that biologically created interests are more important, deserving of more weight on balance, than are experience interests.

THE SOURCE OF BIOLOGICAL SELF-INTEREST

Biological self-interest is derived from the existence and nature of the DNA that creates each individual being on Earth. Inherent and most unique about the nature of the DNA molecule is the fact that it self-replicates, that is, by its biochemical nature it will produce copies of itself. The DNA that is found in living beings consists of special groups of self-replicating molecules that have evolved increasingly complex packages surrounding the molecule that help assure the replication of the next generation of DNA molecules; they are the winners of the battle of evolution.[1]

We are survival machines, but "we" does not mean just people. It embraces all animals, plants, bacteria, and viruses. We are all survival machines for the same kind of replicator—molecules called DNA. Beginning with the simplest life-form, the forces of genetic selection over millions of years have evolved different bodies in shape, size, and ability to support the DNA that pushes for the birth of the next generation.[2] It is one of the amazing aspects of life that a complex molecule that clearly cannot be self-aware has been pushed by evolution to create a body to carry it that can be self-aware.

The domestic cat, the blue bird, the monarch butterfly, the chimpanzee, and the human all come into existence (are born) because of the combining of DNA from an egg and a sperm from their biological parents in a special environment. It is amazing how by changing the code by which the DNA is constructed (which consists of only four distinct variables), such amazingly different packages/bodies are produced. No one can choose what body to be; you simply are the body that you are. The body is of course much more than just the physical structure. Each body or survival machine protects the DNA from environmental harm. Thus, we vertebrates have pain receptors to warn us of external threats. The turkey is born with an eye a bit different from a human's and an instinct to watch the sky. They have a set of brain neurons that quickly sort the incoming visual signals and will call out alarms with the sighting of objects in the sky that might be predators. This is a critical capacity for a turkey in order to survive long enough to produce the next generation. This is an instinct, not some mystical event; it is hardwired in this particular animal by its DNA.

Some bodies learned to breathe oxygen and walk on legs. Some can see the world with color; others smell the world around them. Many DNA bodies have developed the capacity to feel pain, and some of these have a capacity for self-awareness or degrees of consciousness. These diverse bodies carrying their DNA, which we see as the animals around us today, have evolved over millions of years under evolution's rules of natural selection. One of the most complex, and at the moment most successful, packages is that of *Homo sapiens sapiens*, today's humans. Remember that rocks and cars have no DNA and do not have a capacity to self-replicate, and they do not have an interest in so doing. Indeed, they have no interests at all.

DNA-constructed beings have a will to live, will fight to live, and will kill other living beings in order to stay alive. Importantly, it is the balance between life and death that drives the evolution of different life packages. To say that a living being has biological interests is simply to acknowledge that each individual has been endowed by its DNA with a package of skills and capabilities that may be expected to be exercised by the individual in pursuing its life and the creation of the next generation. A primary interest of a bat is that it be in darkness during the day, while the turtle will seek out the sun to raise its body temperature and become fully functional. To deny the turtle the heat of the sun or the bat the flight of the night is to interfere with a fundamental interest of an individual of that species.

As a starting point, some of the behaviors that most, but not necessarily all, animals engage in and that demonstrate the scope of their interests include:

> fighting for continued life,
> finding and consuming food on a regular basis,
> socialization with others (usually of same species),
> mating,
> caring for their young,
> sleeping,
> accessing sunlight (or not),
> exercising their inherent mental capacities,
> moving about in their physical environment.

HUMAN INTEREST

The entire above list also applies to humans. For example, consider how much of human activity is directly or indirectly related to the DNA compulsion to create the next generation, to produce babies and support them until they can be independent. At the primary level there is sexual attraction between individuals and the sex-versus-love tension. At a more abstract level it is why sellers of cars seem to always have attractive women in their commercials. Likewise, most animals invest most of their day in finding and eating the appropriate food, which makes it a primary interest for animals. But for many of us humans food is everywhere, we just need to work to gain the money necessary to buy it.

Human brains are much more complex than other animals', and with that complexity comes the capacity for many more interests. Most of us have at some point said: "I wish I could lead the simple, good life of my dog or cat." No cat or dog will have to figure out what immigration policy the United States should adopt or how to make a democracy work or how to get his daughter to band practice after school while he is stuck at work. The social structure and neurological complexity of humans has given us the invention of farming and gunpowder, to name just two things. Life is indeed fairly simple for our companion animals compared to ours. Not only does the human brain have many, many more neurons to obtain and process information, but because we are one of the few species to go through social group evolution, few other animals have the constant tension of humans who seek to be both an individual and part of a social group. To have social communities requires that some of the members possess those character traits that produce leadership abilities for the group to survive. As an ever-present counterpoint to being part of a group is the desire to be selfish in order to ensure individual survival. Whom to kill or whom to help, on an evolutionary scale, was usually decided by knowing what community an individual was part of, and by recognizing family ties.

One of the things humans did a while ago was to invent money, which is extremely useful for building complex communities. Humans understand clearly the necessity for money in today's world. It is with money that we are able to satisfy first our biologically created interests and then a wide assortment of experience interests (e.g., helping others, racing horses, or collecting beer cans). Reflect for a moment how much of life is focused upon the enterprise of obtaining and spending money and how much of the human character is revealed in this process. Just as sugar, with its DNA-driven roots, has been a problem in the modern world, in which sugar is too abundant, perhaps money has become too available in the modern world as well. Often animals or animal products are used to satisfy these uniquely human interests (e.g., for shoes, burgers, racing animals, and watching animals at zoos). But understand that obtaining money is not really an important interest in itself; it is merely a means to satisfy the real interests of the human individual.

COMMUNITY INTEREST

As discussed in chapter 6, humans are a part of many different communities. In turn, each community is composed of a set of humans. And being composed of humans, a community has within it often-different ideas about how the community should proceed. It is fairly well accepted that it is not unusual that an ultimate decision of a community may run against the best interest of some individuals within the group. A consideration of which communities a person is part of will help identify which experience interests are important to him or her.

With many communities, if an individual disagrees with a community decision, then the person has the option of leaving the community. For example, if a religious group decides to allow/not allow women to have a leadership position, then the individual who disagrees with the decision must decide to stay within the community or leave it. While it is natural to talk about the interests of the community (e.g., a condo association, a specific city, or an organization like the Boy Scouts of America), such interests are really just a cumulative pile of the individual interests of the humans composing the group. I don't have ethical duties toward cities or organizations, but I will have ethical duties toward the humans and animals that are a part of the community. When animals are part of a community, they usually do not have the option of leaving the community, which is one reason why we need to be more aware of just what are the circumstance in which they live.

ENVIRONMENTAL INTERESTS

Can we talk about the environment having interests? Not really, since the environment is primarily a place where beings live, not a being itself. But like a city composed of humans, Yellowstone Park, for example, is a place composed of many, many living beings. We humans often refer to Yellowstone as if it were a being itself, but it is only a shorthand notion used to speak of the cumulative interests of all the inhabitants bundled up together, as well as all of the conflicting interests of the various individuals and the ecology of the place. But, as will be seen later, this shorthand notion will also be useful to us.

CONFLICTS OF INTERESTS BETWEEN HUMANS

Human beings have interests. Sometimes, many times, these interests are in conflict with the interests of other human beings. To help us understand some of the complexities, let us return to Homer, who has an interest in cherry pies; he would love to have a pie every day. There is nothing inherently wrong with this interest, and presumably he is free to fulfill this interest within the limitations of his culinary skill and personal resources. However, if he seeks to satisfy this interest by taking a pie made by Sally Top, without paying or without her permission, then his interest will be in conflict with Sally's interest in either eating the pie herself or in receiving compensation for her labor and cost of materials.

Now the question becomes, Can we make an ethical judgment about this conflict? If Homer takes the pie against the wishes of Sally, is that unethical conduct? Our intuitive answer is yes; the conduct is unethical and should be condemned by right-thinking people. Now is not the time to unpack that judgment, and though the issue seems a bit on the trivial side, the principle is of great significance. Indeed, the principle is a fundamental component of our legal system. Theft is a crime. Human history suggests that protecting someone's work product or invention from theft is a critical component in the keeping of a peaceful society and, therefore, the community has adopted a series of rules/laws to deal with this conflict.

At a less trivial level, Homer may also have an interest in having a social date with Ms. Top. And again Ms. Top's interest may be the opposite. She may have an interest in being free from the attention of Homer. Is his conduct unethical? Assuming that this is a verbal exchange, then it does not seem unethical to ask. Men have been asking forever. This conflict will normally be resolved by Homer and Sally, and indeed thousands of times daily this conflict arises and is resolved without the intervention of the law.[3] If, however, Homer decides to further his interest by touching or grabbing Ms. Top, or perhaps by calling her and following her for days on end, he has exceeded the norms of social conduct. He has interfered with her liberty rights. As such, his conduct has moved into the unethical and perhaps illegal area. The legal recourse for her would be in the form of criminal charges for harassment, battery, or stalking, and the civil right to seek an injunction against further intrusion of her privacy.

CONFLICTS OF INTERESTS BETWEEN HUMANS AND ANIMALS

As a set of examples to show some of the complexity of conflicting interests between humans and animals, please consider the following three scenes in which JoJo, an adult chimpanzee, is the focal point.

1. JoJo lives in the Potsville Zoo. He is one of a group of ten chimpanzees on a three-acre tract that was part of a $6 million project the zoo built three years ago. Zoo visitors can see the chimpanzees from five viewing positions. However, chimpanzees have the ability to retreat out of view if they wish. There is a trained caregiver on duty ten hours a day. The caregiver has the obligation to observe the chimpanzees for medical needs, to provide them with creative food-gathering challenges, to ensure that their individual interactions do not cause harm, to control humans so that they do not do stupid things, and to generally ensure the chimpanzees' well-being. Homer complains to the zoo that regardless of the size of the cage, JoJo is still not able to move about in as large an area as he would in nature, and that the confinement interferes with his fundamental interest in personal freedom. Is the keeping of JoJo in the zoo unethical? This is basically the situation suggested at the beginning of the book. What do you think? Balance the interests of the chimpanzee, the zoo, and the visitors to the zoo. Should it be illegal?

2. JoJo lives in the basement of the home of Big Jones in a commercial cage measuring 5' × 5' × 7'. Big Jones collects exotic animals and shows off JoJo to all his beer-drinking friends by banging on the cage to get a reaction out of JoJo. After several months in residence, JoJo no longer reacts to cage rattling and has cut back on eating the table scraps that Big Jones feeds him. This comes to the attention of Homer, who sends a letter objecting to this possession as unethical conduct by the owner of such a complex being. The fundamental interests of JoJo are clearly at risk. There is no socialization, no physical exercise, no enrichment of the environment, a lack of appropriate food, and clear psychological abuse. JoJo is basically a living trophy for Big Jones. The interests of the owner, Big Jones, are personal: he has a modest financial investment in the animal, and he feels important as the center of atten-

tion within his community of human friends with JoJo in his house. It makes him feel special, providing part of his self-identity and self-esteem. Is the conduct of Big Jones unethical? Balance the interests. Should it be illegal?

3. As a final example, consider JoJo, who has lived for twenty years in an institutional lab at Big University. His cage of iron bars meets the requirements of the federal law, with physical dimensions of 5' × 5' × 7'. However, he never sees the natural light of the sun or the touch of any other chimpanzee. There is nothing for him to do in the cage, no emotional connection with others or activities to provide intellectual focus. He has been part of three different scientific protocols over the past fifteen years. Is this keeping of a chimpanzee unethical by the university or the individual researcher? Does it matter what information has been or might be gained in utilizing this animal in the name of science? Should the question be framed in terms of this particular chimpanzee, or should it be framed in terms of all chimpanzees held at research facilities? Balance the interests.

In example 3, it would not be unusual for the reader to see both sides of the dispute, as both have important values that they represent, making ethical decisions more difficult. This last hypothetical suggests how important but difficult determining the weight of a particular interest will be when making an ethical judgment. Some believe the inquiry of science wins over any interests held by the individual chimpanzee; other humans believe that science could never justify its significant interference with the chimpanzee's fundamental interests in a laboratory-research setting.

One complexity of the third example is that the potential benefit of scientific information could flow to large numbers of humans. But, it is impossible to know in advance of engaging in specific animal experiments what, if any, usefulness the experiment may have, or even when the information might be useful. On the other hand, there is the certainty of the negative impact on the animal used in the experiment. Today it is highly unlikely that a chimpanzee would be the subject of an invasive experiment, because the scientific community has quietly decided that chimpanzees should no longer be used in science.[4] So, to pursue this question of balance between human and animal interests, should experiments be done with a dozen beagles instead of a chimpanzee (or perhaps fifty rats)?

So, if the currency of the discussion is the kind and level of interest, how are we to give value to different kinds of interests? How should we decide about the ethics of the use of animals by humans?

For Their Sake

Pigs and chickens and cows,
Are interesting.
Have interests.
Can we see them?
Can we hear them?
Can we act,
For Them?

CHAPTER 9

PAUSE AND REFOCUS

Since a number of threads of thought have been presented to the reader in the previous chapters, it might be useful to refocus on the key questions of this book. I seek to build an ethical world in which humans limit their use of animals to respectful circumstances. Much of the prior material has been developing information and concepts to help with that most difficult of actions: making a judgment about respectful use. How do we make judgments? What information should be present to make a judgment, and how are we to weigh the competing or conflicting interests of the ethical actor and ethical subject?

Some examples of questions that require an internal ethical discussion include:

Should I put my dog in the crate for the ten-hour day while I am at work?

Should I eat the meat of an unseen pig?

Should I watch a movie that resulted in the death of a horse?

Should I go to the greyhound racetrack and have fun?

Should I go to the zoo?

Should I kick the dog?

Should I buy stock in a company that keeps millions of chickens in caged confinement?

Should I shoot the wild mountain goat to complete my mounted-head collection?

Should I breed my horse, dog, cat, or snake?

These are all ethical questions, although individuals might not initially identify them as such. These questions may well produce a quick judgment—the two-second, unexamined response. Or they may be an opportunity to engage in rational consideration by seeking out information, context, and values. The answer should come only after putting on the table the values important to the human, the animal, and the community that they share. Then the weighing of interests is done within one brain and a decision is made.

As each person develops his or her own frame of reference, it is often useful to see how others are making their animal decisions. Why are other humans more or less respectful of their animals? Do they use an ethical frame of reference at all? Perhaps I can learn from them or teach them something. Ultimately, we can and will judge the actions of others as being ethical or unethical, good or bad, acceptable or unacceptable. This is appropriate, because if their actions are causing harm to animals, then intervention may be necessary, just as it would be necessary to intervene in the affairs of a human family for the well-being of some children. Perhaps if discussion or social pressure fails, laws will have to be passed and enforced.

THE CAT AND THE CACTUS

As I walked through the study one morning, I noticed Willow, our retired barn cat, napping in a splash of sunlight less than a foot from my cactus plant, which was also soaking up some sunlight. It occurred to me that there were great similarities between the two. They are both mine and require my care; they both have prickly points; they take up about the same space; they hang around the house accomplishing nothing in particular except being decorative to our home; and they are both alive. Neither will contribute to the next generation of life on Earth, which is sad. I care for both. Why do I?

If we do not seek to envision the future, it will engulf us as the wave does the sand castles built upon the shore . . .

CHAPTER 10

THE PROCESS OF MAKING JUDGMENTS

Well, how are we doing? Are you still following the tracks of my thoughts? Perhaps you are still reading but holding back any judgment. Let's leave the animal arena for a few pages and consider an important human capacity, that of making judgments (i.e., conclusions, decisions). This is important because the book you are reading is a result of my personal judgment about how to think about animals. It was the result not of a rigorous logical exercise but of the culmination of life experiences and the weight of a thousand events and ideas mushed together in my mind until a judgment was reached. It is useful to understand this because animal issues are not easy; they can be very complex. Many variables and experiences feed into the decision-making. Before we get to what is perhaps the most difficult of judgments, namely, humans supporting, allowing, or causing the death of animals, we need to reflect upon the process of making judgments, understanding that animals also make judgments.

Sometimes we reach a decision and feel strongly about it but may not be able to articulate why we came to that particular decision. I reached a number of decisions about animals after living on my farm with livestock for a period of time. The conclusions I reached at the time could not be well explained to others. Over a number of years since then, I have tried to come to understand myself and to find the words to express to others not just my judgment in this or that situation, but also the why of my judgment. I fear that without understanding the why, many will simply set aside my judgment as not particularly useful. Also, it might be the case that some readers agree or disagree with me as they go through this book, but they cannot exactly say why. I would like to suggest that such a state is acceptable, at least in the short term.

HOW WE THINK

There are reasons for judgments or decisions, but they are not always immediately accessible or expressible in words and sentences. Understanding why this might be the case will be useful. Also, in doing this we will learn a bit more about animals, or at least mammals. This in turn might lead to a more respectful consideration of animals as ethical subjects.

Most people who have companion animals say their animals are part of their family, and as such have a presence in their lives that is different from the beds and tables of their homes. This is a judgment, a conclusion that forms a critical basis for other judgments and decisions. Usually this just happens; it does not arise out of discussions of philosophy or ethics. It is intuitively obvious to pet owners that their pet is different: she is alive—she has wishes, desires, needs, and capacities that have to be acknowledged and accepted, whereas the table in the corner does not. Pet owners believe that an emotional bond can be nurtured between humans and animals. This, of course, is of the same flavor but perhaps not same intensity as the sense of their relationship to their children. It can be emotional, mutual, rewarding, and demanding. Companion animals are actors that join us on the stage of life; they are not mere props to be used without concern as the play of life develops.

What to eat is a judgment. Whether to do an act or not do an act, to kick the dog or hug the dog, is a judgment. Not all judgments have ethical consequences, but many do. But how does this happen; what is the physical activity that produces a judgment? It is more difficult to explain than might first appear to be the case, because we have two sides to our brain and they are not identical in structure and operation. Each side of the brain can make a judgment, and they are sometimes in conflict with each other, as when someone says one thing, and yet does another. When Homer walks in the door and sees objects on the floor (a dog, a ball, and an infant), whatever the action that is taken, it is the result of a judgment in his brain, a judgment that fires neurons that contract muscle groups of the arms and legs, thereby producing the action. Most likely, in less than a second, the judgment will be made and the muscles ordered to carry out the task.

If Homer were a thoughtful ethics professor who was in touch with his emotions, he would come to the door understanding that his emotional hormones have placed him in a negative state of mind. Upon opening the door and seeing the objects on the floor, two of them being ethical subjects (the dog and the infant), he would contemplate the appropriate ethical action for a minute or so, weighing how the universe would judge him, what his wife would say, and what the impact of the various action options might be on the ethical subject, and then he would reach out and give a hug. A rational judgment will take perhaps ten to twenty times longer than the noncontemplative judgment. One is a judgment with words and ideas; the other is without words, but with neurons firing through the brain and a life of experiences as an unstated context.

THE LOGICAL VERSUS THE HOLIST

We adults know much of the world around us, and many of our life experiences have molded the neural network that makes up the physical structure of our brain. Every time we make a judgment, small or large, it is not on a blank slate but within the physical context of our neural network as it exists at the moment of the judgment.

Have you watched a dog make a decision? Or, even better, have you seen a dog regret a decision? I'm not sure what science would say about those two processes, but dogs do makes decisions, and I am sure they did so long before joining up with humans. They do so without using words, sentences, or paragraphs, the tools of language and logical analysis. How is this possible?

Annie, one of our Great Pyrenees, will be out on the driveway when I open the door and ask her, "Do you want to come in for dinner?" Whether or not she understands the specific words, she understands the choice being offered to her: continued freedom to run about or come inside for a bowl of food, a situation she has experienced before with similar gratifying results. It usually takes her about five seconds to make a decision. Her head comes down a little and her eyes may move from me to somewhere else; she is weighing the alternatives, but without words to think about it. Then the decision is made and she either comes trotting toward me or sprints off in another direction. (This is a true choice I am offering her, not a command that she might disobey, which is another analysis altogether.)

Another example of animals thinking is when I have seen my sheep solve a problem. Our land is divided into a number of different fields, and we often want to move the sheep from one field to another. Sometimes they are in field A and, having opened the gate, I am standing in field B, with tall, delicious grasses and clover all around me. I call them to come join me, and they are eager to do so. At first they run directly toward me, but there is a fence between us since the gate may be twenty yards or more away to their right or left. They stop at the fence, and I can see them trying to figure out how to get to the new field and the food it contains. All of a sudden, one or more of them "get it"; the sheep makes a judgment and starts moving right or left along the fence line until one or more of them reach the gate and then run through the gate into the new field. Now, I am sorry to say that some of my sheep do not seem to have the capacity to solve this problem, and I have to go to the gate opening and get them to come to me. Leader sheep consistently reach better decisions quicker than the others. As with humans, sheep, even within a breed, have different levels of intelligence (the capacity to understand the world around them).

How do they do it without words? Fairly easily. They desire something and must make a decision. This should be referred to as animal intelligence: the process by which animals make decisions about what to do or not to do, without the use of words. Are they self-aware of their decision? No, I don't think so, but, then again, we humans often make decisions without being aware of what we are doing.

I suggest that my rejection of the arguments of the abolitionist about the status of animals, Annie's decision about dinner, and the sheep's ability to find the gate occurred by the same neurological process. The full story of how the firing of neuron cells within the mammalian brain creates information, understanding, and action is beyond the scope of this book. While such a full exploration would be fun, it would pull us too far off our path of progress. Instead, I offer a few summary points as a context for our discussion.

OUR BRAINS IN OPERATION

Using words and logically constructed sentences to describe a thousand points of simultaneous analysis, and the information exchange and memory processes that physically change the structure of the brain day by day, is very difficult to describe and comprehend. Here are but a few points about what the brain is doing on an average day.

Our brain is the place where two worlds interact. First is the external world, which we are aware of through the sensory cells of the eyes, nose, throat, ears, and skin (touch, texture, and temperature). This raw sensory information is initially processed by the brain into a more useful form and then is sent on to other parts of the brain. (For the moment, the logic center will be considered that portion of the brain that has the speech center with all the associated words, the left side of the brain. The holistic center is another portion of the brain that is capable of receiving input, making decisions, and acting on them, but without reliance on words, on the right side of the brain.) While simplistic, it is useful to think of the two sides of the brain as two distinct neuron networks working in parallel and sharing some information, but performing different types of analysis on the information that it has. One aspect has full access to words, language, and grammar; the other does not, which is more representative of how other mammalian brains work. The human capacity for storing information and abstractions as word groups is, if not unique, unsurpassed by the other animals of the planet.

The internal world of our own body has another, more primitive method of communication, that of sending hormone messages by way of the blood system. Our brains are constantly awash in these messages, which are produced in times of fear, hunger, sexual desire, thirst, and other bodily interests. This information is initially delivered to the brain by the blood network that connects our internal organs to the brain, rather than the neuron network that delivers information about the external world. Hormones can act at the points of synaptic signal transfer to boost the strength of the neuron signal, or to block a signal, or to affix to the body of a neuron to trigger the firing of the neuron. When Annie, our dog, is faced with the decision about whether or not to come into the house when given the option to eat, it is a decision in which hormones play a big part. Is the stomach sending a hormone message to the brain, directing her toward food? How tired is she? Will the adrenaline rush of a possible cat chase be stronger than the hunger signal? What does my tone of voice suggest about my intentions toward her? Some memory association will also be present. Does going in the house represent a positive or a negative experience? There may be twenty variables that go into the one decision about coming into the house. Within one brain, the context for judgments will always be a mixture of the existing neuron network (representing genes and past experiences); hormones (representing immediate information about the internal world of the being); and the information flowing though the neuron network about the external world, as experienced at that moment.

Neurons within the brain both process and store information about the external world, and can form associations with internal information. If Annie is always fed inside the house, then hunger satisfaction is associated with going into the house. The brain then can use the pattern (prior experience) as a piece of operative information.

The sheep trying to get to the new grass is an example of prior mental associations overcoming the immediate emotional state that is driving the sheep to the new grass. First the sheep reach a fence or see the fence and understand from prior experience that they cannot go through the wire of the fence. (Lambs, on the other hand, have to learn this experience; it is not genetically encoded.) But prior experience suggests to them that I would not be calling them if there were no access. Those that have gone through the specific gate in question are faster in realizing the answer to the problem of how to get to the grass. I do not believe that they have words in their brains with which they think through the problem. It is done in the holistic center of their brains without a word being used to aid analysis.

At any moment the mammalian brain is processing information at thousands of different points within the brain. It is as if there are thousands of computers with limited tasks going about their jobs of processing input signals and sending output on to others—multiple numbers of computers that in turn process input from a variety of links within the brain. But we humans are unaware of the vast majority of this activity.[1] We are not "aware" of the neurons that constantly scan incoming visual information for movement in the field of vision, but if unusual movement is detected, a signal is sent to the conscious part of the brain to "get our attention." While we are doing many things at the same time within the brain, our conscious thoughts are limited to just one train of thought. The physical attributes of human consciousness are not clear, but it appears that the language and logic center have a firm grip on its operation. However, remember that consciousness is just one of many processing centers within the brain.

RESPECTING ANIMALS

The more primal process of mammalian decision-making is based upon multiple-point simultaneous evaluation of information without words and paragraphs. I needed a tag to describe this non-word-related processing of information and have been using the phrase "holistic" decisions or judgments to capture this processing. It is through holistic judgments that mammals make their decisions, as described above for Annie and the sheep. Other vertebrate animals also likely have this structural capacity, but for the purposes of this book there is no need to find the line in the animal kingdom below which it does not exist. Dogs, sheep, and humans share a brain organization with different degrees of capacity.

Likewise, we humans can come to know and accept things without being able to articulate in sentences why or how we do so. Indeed, some of the most important judgments in a person's life are holistic in nature. Does my wife love me? Should I kiss her? Whom should I vote for? Is there a god? Holistic judgments most certainly make use of information, but the information is not necessarily processed as sentences or accessible by the use of tag words. The love of another may be discerned by the look on a face or the touch of a hand and understood and acted upon by a person, with the words coming later. Holistic processing is a multi-tracked and multi-threaded process with multiple focal points.

The alternative process for human decision-making, using words and sequences of sentences, will be referred to as a "logic" judgment. Is the killing of a human wrong? While someone could give an immediate, simple yes or no answer (which would necessarily be a holistic response), it is also possible to suggest a logical sequence of sentences that supports the ethical position that the killing of another human is wrong. Such an argument is built with words, associated with patterns, and processed with logic.

Note that logical analysis is as slow as the thinking of the words. We can think faster than we can speak, so sentence-driven logical judgments are slow in comparison to multi-tracked holistic thinking. On the other hand, the examination of a sequence of logical sentences can be recorded, recalled, and considered one by one to see if they are reasonable. A holistic judgment can be much more difficult to take apart and examine, because many events happened simultaneously and were never reduced to words. So both a human and a dog can make a near-instant choice about important decisions. While humans can internally reexamine prior judgments days or years later, I don't think my dogs or sheep can ponder a prior action.

Now, what might all of this have to do with my rejection of the abolitionist position that no animal should be used by humans, and acceptance of my ram Jet's position that life under my care is acceptable? In the early 2000s, I heard and understood the abolitionists' logic but rejected their conclusions that animals should not be property and should not be used by humans. I could not say why initially; at the time, it was a holistic judgment. My rejection occurred first outside the logic and language center of conscious thought, and we need to understand that this is not only possible but important. Indeed, there had to be a time when our human ancestors did not have language, but they still had to be able to think and to make decisions, or they would not have survived. Just because humans developed language skills and a specialized area of the brain to create and understand word tags does not mean that the original pre-language decision-making ability of our brain has been removed. I believe that non-sentence-based decision-making not only is still available to us but also is critical to being human.

There are some serious limits to our capacity to engage in logical thinking. The most serious limitation is how many variables can be considered when making a logical judgment, particularly when each variable has differing levels of credibility and probability. (Very low-probability events are the most difficult to deal with logically, but that is not particularly important for this discussion.) Even more confusing is where there may be feedback relationships between the variables, either positive or negative. We humans do fine with a few alternatives, but we quickly reach a point of complexity beyond which sentences are no longer helpful. For instance, long-range weather forecasts exist only because computers can do that which the human mind cannot.

Consider the issue facing a sheep breeder of a modest flock: Which of her four rams should be mated with which of her twenty-five ewes? Since much financial, physical, and emotional effort will be required in dealing with the offspring, the question is important. Twenty-nine sheep are a modest number, but if you do a little math, you realize that over a hundred different pairings are possible. Most of them would not be optimal from a sheep breeder's perspective. To sort out the best alternatives, there are a number of factors to consider:

1. General health of each animal.
2. Fleece color and pattern (three different sheep genes produce variable outcomes).
3. Horn shape, size, and genetic history.
4. Prior mating outcomes and prior birthing experiences.
5. Relatedness of individual sheep to one another.
6. Market interests in obtaining particular fleeces and wool patterns.
7. Breed standards about fleece quality, horn directions, straightness of the back legs, and other factors.

When my wife and I discuss all these factors, we quickly become lost in our logical analysis. No mathematical formula will answer the questions. Either the number of logical variables must be reduced, or we must use a holistic judgment, or, as with many human decisions, we combine both approaches. Thus, Marty and I consider the ewe named Misty. Should she be bred at all? Is she related to any of the rams? If so, how far back? Do we want a fleece-focused outcome for her? Or should conformation, or color patterns dominate the decision? She has strong horns, so we might be able to use a ram with weaker horns. But the ram is related to her by one parent three generations back, and the last time we bred him, he produced only black offspring. With another ram, Misty might produce black-gray lambs; and so it goes, on and on with each possibility. By the day that the breeding groups are put together, the decisions have been made. One hundred and forty some days later, the consequences of those decisions begin to be revealed.

Figure 10.1.

Sometimes humans come to a judgment and are willing to act on it even when they cannot say why they did so: "I am leaving my wife; she no longer loves me." "I froze in my tracks until the dog passed." "I knew I would get the job offer." "That performance of Beethoven was not a good one, I am leaving." "This is a beautiful painting; let's buy it."

A baseball player is standing at home plate, bat in hand, waiting for the pitch. Should he swing at this pitch? If so, how should he swing? There is no time for an internal logical discussion; it is a holistic decision. We might say it was instinct. But the decision to swing or not swing the bat is the result of a holistic judgment somewhere in the brain; arms do not move of their own accord. Some portion of the brain triggered the necessary motor neurons, causing the muscles in the arm to move. It was unlikely to be a random event. Similarly, when a woman picks out a set of fabrics for a quilt, she may or may not be able to articulate, in sentence form, how each judgment comes about. The decision may be a mixture of sentence-driven thoughts composed of words and unconscious holistic judgments about color and texture.

Returning to our dog, Annie, and remembering that dogs do not have language centers as humans do, consider how she might process the event of a familiar man approaching her. Annie would recognize his shape, and possibly his scent, but she would not be able to produce a name tag for the person. Annie's response may be to advance gleefully, turn and run, cower, or just hold steady. The response/decision is the result of a holistic judgment. While the dog does not have a name for the approaching man, she does have associated memories that may well include the events that followed his approach in the past. Perhaps the place of the current encounter, or what the man is holding in his hand, or the look on his face, or Annie's level of hunger will change her response. Again, many variables can be at work within the brain at any one point in time. The response is not random or the result of genetic hardwiring of the brain. (We need to distinguish between the action options available to a particular animal, which may be genetically limited, and the decision about which option to use, which is usually not genetically hardwired in mammals.) Most likely, it is rational within the context of the dog's experiences. But, of course, she cannot explain her reaction to us.

HOLISTIC JUDGMENTS WITHIN THE LAW

As a final example of holistic thinking, consider the world of law, which normally gives high priority to logical analysis. Often, the person who best constructs a logical analysis will win a legal argument. But even within our legal structure there exist important examples of holistic judgment. One is the jury system. For hundreds of years, a critical component of conflict resolution between the state and an individual has been to put the decision of the most critical factual determinations into the hands of non-lawyers, of average citizens without special knowledge. A trial by jury is logic-driven for the most part, with the lawyers arguing and presenting evidence, while the judge directs the jury's attention toward and away from evidence. But, the jury represents a built-in restraint upon the logic-driven legal process because the jury possesses the power to reject a logical analysis and apply a holistic judgment: "He's guilty" or "He's innocent." Thus, weeks of testimony are reduced to a simple one-word judgment. One of the reasons we rely upon the jury system for justice is that logic and sentences do not always arrive at the most appropriate judgment. Experienced prosecutors and defense lawyers understand the power and willingness of juries to make holistic judgments, and they support that process, while also providing the logical analysis for the court and subsequent appeals within the legal system.

The legal system never demands a jury's decision be justified by the members of the jury either by written or spoken word. It is often a fruitless question to ask of the individual members of a jury for their justification of their decision. This is why the interviews with members of juries after a trial often seem flat; they cannot always explain their decisions. So, even within the legal system, there is space for both kinds of decision-making. In the creative arts, the antithesis of the law, holistic judgments are dominant, with logic playing only a supporting role. This process will be seen again in the legal system when the phrase "unjustified pain and suffering" is considered as our social standard for the treatment of animals. Just what does that mean to a person sitting on a jury?

It has been my experience that many will accept only a logic-driven analysis. But my initial judgment about the acceptability of the use of my farm animals was holistic. It was over the next few years that I worked out a way of articulating in sentences my perspective and the supporting arguments for this judgment. With this book I seek to communicate with readers both by using logical analysis and by other means.

RESPECTING ANIMALS

Judgments

Am I right,
Am I wrong?

Is a leap of
Faith
Without reason?

Do words,
Stop you,
Start you?

Does reason
Rule?
Do feelings
Trump?

Within me
Within you.

Within us
Minds of
Frightening
Complexity.

Yet,
Every day, we
Muddle through.

JUDGMENTS AND INFORMATION

It is fully appropriate in the midst of having a logical discussion to realize that more information is needed before a judgment can be made. It is more difficult when a holistic judgment is made. When a holistic judgment is made, at least four different factors will be an active part of the judgement:

1. Prior experiences that have shaped the neuron network of the mind
2. Information that is stored in memory
3. The mix of hormones existing in the brain at the time of the judgement
4. The information of the external world as provided by the senses (e.g., vision and hearing)

Sometimes a person pauses, feeling something might be wrong, and then considers "Do I have all the information I need?" It is the unusual case when a holistic judgment is put on hold while more information is sought out. For nonhuman animals this is almost impossible; they make holistic decisions with the information at hand. If an animal makes a bad decision, then that will go into the memory and aid the animal the next time it is faced with a similar decision. Our sheep have never raised a hoof and asked for more information.

We know much that we cannot speak.

LIMITS OF LOGIC

Logic is the critical tool of science and technology. It is important to the development of philosophy, but not religion. It is a way of organizing information and ideas. It supports truth seeking. But it is only a process; it is on its face value neutral. It is a tool or a means, not an end. An action cannot be considered good simply because it is logical. Logic cannot provide the importance or the weight of an ethical subject's interests. Once a value system and context is established, then logic is a critical tool for assessing a path forward. It is that part of the mind or brain that informs us about our personal sense as well as a community sense of value and weight, not the logical word center of the brain. Often what are referred to as judgments of the heart have really an acknowledgment that some judgments arise in other parts of the brain and are not those that arise in the logic center.

In the initial discussion of Homer's dilemma, we compared a ball, a dog, and a child. Consider the following logic analysis. The ball is blue, the dog is blue (assume this fact is correct), and the child is brown. Is the dog more like the child or the ball? Since both the ball and dog are blue, then the dog is more like the ball than the child. There is something odd about the logic of the prior sentence; what is odd is the premise that color is relevant to anything I might care about. The statement is not wrong; it is simply not helpful. Picking the premises is what is critical. What if I had chosen being alive as the important criteria in that discussion, or how about the number of legs, or eye color, or weight? Would that have produced better outcomes of analysis?

The logic of equality of all humans is tempered by our genetic predisposition, which says that community, not equality, is critical. We in the United States fight that tension all of the time when developing public policy. That each human is equal is an ideal, but we live in different communities. And we are comfortable in our communities, regardless of the logic that often governs our reasoning. Color of skin should make no difference in how we treat others, but it often does. Progress is made not by the demands of logic but by understanding, expanding, and realigning what "community" means to individual humans.

Some in the animal-rights movement argue that since animals and humans both can experience pain, they are alike, and, thus, animals must be treated the same as humans. The premises are true to a large degree, but the conclusion is not helpful, because the premise, unstated, is that the only thing that counts in ethical analysis is receptivity to pain. This logic is simply unhelpful since there are many other factors that need to be part of the analysis. Beware of this simple logic. When dealing with living things, nothing is simple.

The logic of using chimpanzees in scientific research, since they are so much like us, is the argument of the scientist. But because they are like us, how can we require chimpanzees to spend a lifetime of solitary existence in a 5' × 5' × 7' lab cage and endure all sorts of intrusive and often-invasive tests? Their use by science can only be explained if the scientists hold the position that chimpanzees are not ethically relevant subjects that deserve the consideration of respectful use. The logic-driven scientists will discount the holistic judgments of others that chimpanzees do deserve our ethical concern in favor of the scientific research benefits they provide, until they have a change of heart and see these animals as being ethical subjects.

HABIT VERSUS JUDGMENT

Alas, notwithstanding all that has been explained above, there is another piece of the puzzle. Humans often engage in actions, or inactions, without making a judgment. They do something simply because they have done it before or because their parents or friends have done it before. In more egregious instances, maybe they saw someone do it on YouTube or on television. In such cases, the actions are both unthinking and unexamined. This is of particular importance when examining the use of animals by humans. Someone crops the ears of their dog because their parents did. Or they keep their dog in a cage in the backyard because that is how their dogs were housed when they were children. Others may use live rabbits to test cosmetics because it is considered standard practice in the industry. Still others eat chicken eggs because everyone around them does, and has in the past, so why not?

How much of life is spent doing unexamined activities? If a young man beats the dog that pees on the floor because, as a child, he saw his father beat their family dog for the same act, there is a high risk that it will become an unthinking habit of this man's son as well. If he is not confronted by someone or some event that demands of him, "Why are you doing this?" it may become ingrained as acceptable conduct, and his attitude of physical dominance over his dog will carry over into interactions with other dogs and animals. Half the battle for the respectful use of animals is simply instilling in an individual's head that threshold of thoughtful examination of an issue: Why are you doing this? Remember that respect must arise deep within the thoughts and memories of each individual; it cannot arise by yelling at someone or imposing it by majority vote.

The law will seek to impose limits and direct human conduct. Perhaps it will also help individuals form good habits, but likely without the important component of internal self-reflection.

So, do you know why you do what you do? Think about something you do regularly because you decided to do it verses something you do but don't really know why.

The other side of the coin is that respectful use can be an unthinking habit as well. How you care for your first dog or cat will most likely follow what you saw and experienced as a child. If it was respectful use, you are most likely to do the same. When at age twenty-one you have an ethical discussion with yourself and decide that you are not going to eat eggs from a confinement chicken facility, and stop buying those eggs, you will form a habit. Avoidance will just happen without having to make a judgment every time you are in a store. We humans would be frozen into inaction if every day we had to examine the ethical consequences of everything we do. One self-reflective internal discussion per week would be great. Create a habit of it. The mere act of engaging in one ethical contemplation of an animal issue may change how you see the world.

> Your life is the sum total of the judgments you make as they pile up one on top of another.

CHAPTER 11

VALUES

What is the value of being raised in a positive, protective, and strong family? What is the value of a human life? What about a snake's life? How about the value of one hundred shares of Apple stock? What is the value of parents' love for their children? The term "value" has different meanings that are important to this discussion. As a noun it can mean either "the monetary worth of something" or "relative worth, utility, or importance." As a verb, it can mean either "to estimate or assign the monetary worth" or "to rate or scale in usefulness, importance or general worth."[1]

Making judgments about ethical outcomes requires a balancing of interests between the ethical actor and the ethical subject. This, in turn, requires the weighing of the value of the interests that might be in conflict. And therein lies the problem, since not all value is reducible to money; indeed, some of the most important values cannot be monetized. Value is in the eyes of the beholder. Or, more formally stated, value is the outcome of a subjective, holist judgment within one person's mind as the person weighs the relative importance of action and inaction. If individuals live in the same context or community, and have had the same life experiences, then it is possible that they would hold certain activities to have the same basic value. We all put a high value on our own lives and a bit less on that of strangers. But of course strangers value their own lives more than they value yours. How about your dog or cat verses another person's dog or cat? Value is relative to the individual making the judgment.

If the human ethical actors see an animal only in a monetary sense, and not as an ethical subject, then the value of the animal is likely only to be a market value, dead or alive. For example, what is the value of a winning racehorse to the surrounding humans? That may differ depending on whom we are talking about. Mr. Buggy may have followed the exploits of the horse named Winner from the time of her first race, and has an emotional attachment to the animal. Miss Prim may have helped raise Winner and considers her a loving companion. Ms. Trainer may have formed a close bond with Winner in their years of working together. As these individuals interact with the horse, their sense of the value of the horse to them will affect judgments when they have to make an ethical decision about the horse. It is difficult to compare the value of a relationship with an animal to the value of the money it represents. However, nonmonetary values can trigger action and emotion and thus have existence in the real world.

But on the larger social and economic scale, these values are often discounted because it is the value of the horse to the owner that has the dominant position. The owner may well only see the horse as an asset capable of generating money. In the owner's mind, the money that the horse can generate is paramount. And our capitalist economic system reinforces this view of value.

The legal system is most comfortable with economic value and has always acknowledged it. Additionally, the law acknowledges the relationship between the horse and its owner but no others. Whereas the ethical map around Winner may be complex, with many players, the law sees only the horse and its owner, which greatly simplifies the web of interests to a binary relationship. This also poses a problem.

What about the horse herself; what does Winner value? Here we have to speak for the horse and assume that we understand the nature of the horse and what is important for her well-being. The seeking of money is not within the interests of a horse; it is an abstraction not within the animal's capacity to understand. But the horse will have interests in what money can buy: good oats and hay, water, shelter from the weather, companions (of both the two- and four-legged sort), attention, and a chance to run like the wind. We may assume that Winner has some level of emotional attachment to both Miss Prim, who raised her, and Ms. Trainer. A horse may well enjoy running, and some might even understand the positive nature of winning a race, but I am not sure about that. Thus, it is hard to say whether Winner has an interest in winning rather than just running a race. However, we can conclude that an absentee owner is of no particular value to the horse. The animal does not understand that it is the owner's bank account that provides the people and resources that are important to the horse.

What if the owner of Winner receives an offer to buy the horse for a million dollars? Would it be ethical to sell the horse to Mr. Bragger and take her away from those humans who value her in nonmonetary ways? What if Winner's owner has knowledge that Mr. Bragger knows nothing about horses and that he is hoping Winner will win a few more races so that he can put her up for sale again and make a profit? Mr. Bragger is simply taking a risk in purchasing the horse in the hope of increasing its future value, just like buying Apple stock on Wall Street.

Whether or not selling the horse to Mr. Bragger is an ethical question will first depend upon whether the owner believes Winner is an ethical subject requiring an ethical judgment. If he does not, then it is simply a business transaction and money is the dominant value in making the decision to sell. If the owner does see Winner as an ethical subject, then Winner's interests should come into play. The owner may also understand that the sale impacts other human ethical subjects such as Miss Prim and Ms. Trainer. Now making a judgment becomes much more difficult because none of the interests of the other humans or of Winner can be translated into money. It will not be, it cannot be, an accounting determination. The owner will be making a holist judgment.

This tension between economic and noneconomic values exists in the context of both the individual making a simple decision and in the broadest public policies that a country may face.[2] Should a town zone out Walmart in hopes of keeping an economically vibrant downtown, even if it means that the goods bought in the town will be more expensive than the price Walmart charges? (With the Internet replacing brick and mortar stores, the zoning question may become moot; watch out for Amazon, not Walmart, as the small shop killer.) What is the value to a circus of having an elephant as part of the show? How do we balance the value of the exotic animals to the bottom line of the circus against the poor quality of life for the elephants that are used in the circus? What if the circus were to go bankrupt and thirty people lose their jobs if legal prohibitions take away the big cats and elephants? Then again, what if the crowds diminish and attendance drops because many in the public object to the use of big cats and elephants, and the circus were forced to close down?

Viewing the Moral Universe

Peering out at the world.
Believing it can be only what I see
For me.

Yet one day the
Question arises:
As the bubbles of
A mud pot, unbeknownst
Unsolicited;
Might value be
Beyond my view?

Am not I the determinator
Of value?

But every day I see more,
Unseen the day before.
Can I accept that
There is always
More?

Have I
The view of the child,
Selfish, narrow,
Inexperienced,
Self-focused?

Perhaps,
The worth of the world is
Independent of me.
It exists regardless of
What I am or see.

Value is not just for
Those like me.
But for all that
Be Alive.

THE ENVIRONMENT

The prior discussion had individual animals as a focal point. This is fine for domestic animals, but what about wild animals, which are unknown to humans and therefore unnamed beings? We often refer to humans within their community groups without knowing any particular human or even how many humans might be there. The population of Russia or New Zealand might be referred to in a discussion, as might the brown bears of Alaska. But environmental value is different from just knowing the numbers of different species within a geographic area. To speak of the environmental value is to consider the interactions of a place with the living beings that inhabit it. This value reflects the capacity of a place to sustain a diversity of life. Environmental values exist independent of humans, but humans can decrease or enhance the environmental value of a place at a particular point in time. Environmentalists often try to convince others of the importance of saving natural areas by reducing the natural environmental value to economic terms relating to flood control, clean air, or water quality. Sometimes it works, sometimes not.

Consider a corporation that owns one hundred acres of land outside St. Louis, Missouri, along the Mississippi River. The corporation seeks to create an industrial center to take advantage of the barge traffic along the river. Construction of the facilities will cost $10 million and will employ two hundred individuals, with a total annual payroll of $5 million. The local government is hungry for such an investment. Is this an ethical decision or just an economic one? What is the environmental value at risk? If the hundred acres is presently a cornfield, then the existing environmental value is very small, as cornfields are deserts of life, with the economic value of corn having come to trump all natural value the field might have. To turn this into an industrial center may only modestly change the environmental value of the area.

If the hundred acres is natural fields and forest with a wetlands edge on the river, then the environmental value could be great. If the view is from that of the entire Mississippi River basin, then such a small portion is of relatively no importance. But to the animals that live there, it is everything. How many rabbits, snakes, frogs, birds, raccoons, or opossums use that land? What if it is a part of a key access corridor to the river for the surrounding square miles? What if it is the biggest wetlands area left along this portion of the river? Now what is its value? Does the corporation or the local government take this into account? Does the corporation make an ethical decision about how its project will disrupt the mice and birds that live on the land? Can the ecological existence and value of the mice and birds stand up to a $10 million investment?

The law may direct or channel the decision-making of the corporation, for environmental value is acknowledged within our law. The national Clean Water Act may well require a permit and protect from destruction any wetlands that might be present. Society has made a social judgment that wetlands are a natural environment of such high value that their destruction will be allowed only if a permit is granted by the government. Environmentalists don't usually think of this as an ethical controversy; rather, to them it is an environmental ecological controversy, but it is an ethical one as well. To destroy that field and forest area is conflicting with the primary interests of all the individual beings present in living their life and propagating the next generation. How should we weigh the interest of the corporation in engaging in positive economic activity that will support hundreds of human beings against the interests of the animal inhabitants of the land in question? Do they get respect? Yes, but only sometimes.

The presence of an ethical duty as relates to an ecosystem is not toward the rocks and water that exist, but to the individual beings that live in and near that place. The rocks and water are important to preserve as habitat, food, and shelter, but the focus should be on the living animals of that place. It is useful shorthand for everyone to use when a duty of environmental protection is suggested, but it is really a duty for the preservation of a specific set of lives.

There is another noneconomic value that should be raised at this point. What about endangered species? Does the fact that an individual animal is a member of a species that science has determined is endangered—that is, at risk of extinction—give that animal value beyond the value of the life of the individual animal himself, the other animals in the same area, or the humans who could benefit from the use of the land? Would or should we do more to protect and preserve an animal of an endangered species than one of a non-endangered species? While there is disagreement about this, many individuals would answer yes, we have an extra duty of respect when an individual is of an endangered species. Thus at times the wolf and eagle have obtained special legal protection in the lower forty-eight states of the United States after being listed as endangered by the federal government under the Endangered Species Act.[3]

Where does this bonus value come from? Perhaps it is respect for the fact that this thread of DNA evolved and survived on Earth for a million years or more, and that we humans should seek to preserve all threads of life simply for what they are. A species represents one thread of evolution, one successful strategy for survival, for living one generation after another. Additionally, the value can be boosted with the realization that as species go extinct, the interconnected threads of a place, an ecosystem, are weakened and are less able to support the diversity of life that would otherwise be present. From the human view of time, there is a significant difference between the killing of an individual animal and the killing of an entire species of animals. To the animals themselves it is not different. An individual animal has the same interest in preserving its own life whether or not it is part of an endangered species. Recognition of endangered species is a human category. It is a value we acknowledge in the abstract levels of human thought, that exists apart from us; it should give extra weight to the valuation of individual life when making ethical decisions that impact endangered animals.

What if the corporation's project land suggested above had a dozen turtles of an endangered species living on the land? Does that change the weight of the interests of the animals when deciding whether or not to preserve their habitat? In the United States it does. If the land in question is within the critical habitat of the turtle, then it may be impossible to proceed with the project because of the federal Endangered Species Act.[4] This law was passed because of the social decision that protection of species from extinction outweighs, or is more valuable than, the economic gain that might be realized from the death of the animals, or destruction of their habitat. It is a noneconomic value recognized by individuals and the law.

Grass

Grass is good.
Grass grows green.
Grass is for me,
How about you?

You want a sweater,
Start with grass.
You want an aquifer,
Go with grass.

You want a fox,
Start with grass.
Revitalize the buffalo,
Go with grass.

Capture some CO_2
Release some O_2
Go Grass Go.

There hides the mouse,
There is captured the sun,
There stops the water.

Two-inch tufts
Along the mountain trail.
Eight-foot stalks in
The stream's vale.

Grow some grass.
The Wave flows green.
Go Grass Go.

We would be what
Without the grass?

Thus we leave the discussion of value with the realization that both monetary and nonmonetary values will weigh in the judgment process. It has to be acknowledged that nonmonetary values are very personal and sometimes difficult even to articulate. However, judgments must be and are made. It is now time to work through a few as examples of what can happen.

CHAPTER 12

ETHICAL JUDGMENTS ABOUT ANIMALS

MAKING PRIVATE JUDGMENTS

Let's suppose that Ms. Maple has three cats that live with her in a nice apartment in New York City. She has just received an invitation to visit a friend on Martha's Vineyard for a four-day weekend, but she cannot take the cats. She must make a judgment about what to do with the cats. We hope that the judgment is ethical and respectful. She could put out a big bowl of water, open a bag of dry food to leave on the floor, and lock the door on the way out. The cats, most likely, would be alive when she returned, but most certainly not happy. In Ms. Maple's mind, that judgment may be considered respectful and ethical. The acts are not illegal, since she is providing a minimum level of care. Should someone have a discussion with her to try to change her mind?

Alternatively, Ms. Maple may be able and willing to place the cats in a nice cat hotel, with playtime paid for, at the sum of $100 per day per cat. Is one option respectful and the other not? If the big money is spent, does it mean she is more respectful? If she does not have the money to spend, does that make keeping them at home less respectful?

Remember that respect comes in many different colors and is an individual judgment based upon the person's information, resources, and experience. It is subjective. One measure of respect is how well it accommodates the interests of the animals in question. Would four days in the apartment impose risk of harm for these cats? Well, it depends on the cats. Are these highly social young cats that expect human interactions every day? Or are they rescue cats that mostly stay in a bedroom every day and do not seek out human companionship? In my experience, most cats could handle a few days without human social interactions. But what if the water bowl was tipped over or the food bag fell shut against the wall? It seems to me that four days without any humans looking in on them to make sure all is well is too long. Something could go wrong, something totally unforeseeable. It is were up to me, I would say that the appropriate level of respect would require at least having a human stop in to see what is happening each day. On the other hand, the exotic food and silk pillows of a pet hotel are not necessary for a showing of respect. Should I try to talk with her? How could I change her mind?

What if she had three Australian sheep dogs or German shepherds instead of cats? They are different from cats; respect requires more effort on the part of Ms. Maple because the dogs have more demanding needs. Also, remember that respect is always in relationship to the individual animals in question and the context or community in which the animals and the humans exist. These issues are placed in the community of companion animals.

What if Ms. Maple decided to visit a local zoo, let's call it Sunshine and Roses Zoological Park, which charged a $25.00 admission fee? Is it ethical for her to support this zoo with her money? Once she learns of the facility, she might say to herself: "Does this zoo treat its animals with respect? If not, I will not go, because I do not want to support an organization that is disrespectful of the animals that are in its care." Perhaps she has no information about how the animals are kept. She will gain information while attending and afterward, without detailed reflection, she may simply say, "I am uncomfortable with the small cages I saw the animals being kept in. I don't think I will go back." Such a thought is an ethical judgment, a holistic one, that is, the quick judgment without a sentence-based analysis.

ETHICAL JUDGMENTS ABOUT ANIMALS

What about the zoo: have the zookeepers made good ethical decisions about their animals? They may have made a financial decision that they can make money by reducing their costs using small cages and hope that most people don't notice or care about the cage size. The zoo director or zoo board has a mixture of decisions to make: financial, ethical, and legal. The ethical questions may be the most difficult: *Does the law allow us to obtain the big cats we want to display?* Both federal and state law will be consulted. *Can we secure enough income to cover the daily cost of operation? Where will the animals come from? Can their capture be accomplished in an ethical and respectful manner?* But this last question cannot be forced upon the zoo operators by outsiders because the zoo owners may not even see the animals as ethical subjects, and therefore not believe an ethical question is even before them. As an outsider, I would say that financial goals should be considered only after a baseline of respectful care is provided to the animals. If the zoo cannot provide respectful care, then it should not continue to exist.

Sunshine and Roses Zoological Park is one enterprise within the animal/human community that uses animals for entertainment. Among the leaders of this zoo community in the United States there is a high level of concern for animals and their well-being, both physical and mental. (Often this concern is greater than the law requires.) Therefore, the ethically acceptable bar for treatment by zoos is high and a number of places displaying animals for the public to view do not meet this bar. This is particularly true of roadside zoos with just a few animals; in these cases, the animals are really just eye candy to get the driver to stop at the commercial store that is holding the animals.[1] In the zoo community, rather than focusing on socialization with humans, as is the case in the community of companion animals, the focus is on respecting their wild nature and trying to provide habitats that allow the animals to experience an environment that accommodates their genetically driven interests. (For example, heat level, humidity, cover against the elements, and food acquisition.) This ethical approach will be costlier for the zoo and may not be required by the law, but it is still the "right" thing to do.

RESPECTING ANIMALS

As previously discussed, our intellectual framework for rational, logical discussion is respectful use. Let us return to the example that started the book. When Homer walks in the door of his home and decides whether to kick and what to kick, it is a holistic judgment arrived at within a few seconds. There will not be time for rational contemplation with words and sentences. If respect for the dog does not preexist before he walks in the door, then it is doubtful that it will be realized at that moment. The holistic judgment is dependent upon previously stored information and judgments (habits) toward living beings. Now, if Homer does kick the dog and the dog cries out in pain, then Homer, one hopes, will have a rational discussion with himself about what happened, that it was wrong, and that in the future he will show enhanced respect for his pets. Now, when the urge to strike out comes upon him in the future, he will come to a different holistic judgment and not kick the animal. This is called being human.

MAKING COLLECTIVE JUDGMENTS

In 2008, an undercover video taken by the Humane Society of the United States was released showing the pushing of a downed cow by a bulldozer at a slaughterhouse. Anyone who sees this footage most likely will make an immediate, holistic judgment that the human treatment of the animal in this film is ethically wrong, whether or not it was illegal.[2] It does not matter that in thirty minutes the animal will be killed to provide food for humans; in fact, in some ways that makes the issue even more important. (The video and resulting public reaction provide the political impulse for changing the law to make it clear that such conduct is unacceptable in our society.) This is an example of individual ethical decisions coming together with one vision or voice and creating a group ethical decision. There is no need for a scientific expert to discuss the matter, and no defense could possibly be offered up by the actors. It is also an example of what most individuals would categorize as disrespectful—if not down-right cruel—actions by a human to an animal. Some decisions do not need a logical analysis.

The pictures of the clubbing of baby seals on the Canadian ice flows bring the same sort of revulsion to most viewers: it is unacceptable conduct. The death of the young, the spattering of blood, the mother seals in anguish, give all the clues necessary to trigger a negative holistic judgment in the viewer. (For a sample of this visceral public impact, type "seal clubbing" into YouTube's search bar.) Being offered the additional information that the person needs the seal pelts to make money and that death by crushing the brain is sometimes near instantaneous for the seal pup does not sway us from this judgment. The human interests do not seem to overcome the overwhelming visual impact of what is happening to specific individual baby seals.

Yes, emotion is part of the judgment, but whether we acknowledge it or not, emotions have always been part of the judgment-making process. Sometimes emotions will lead us places that on balance we should not go, and in such instances the logic center acts as counterpoint to the holistic, quick response. Road rage is an example of emotion resulting in a bad outcome. But the logic center may not be able to take charge until after the heat of the moment. (That is one reason we have so many humans in jail. When asked about why a convicted person acted as they did, a common response is: "It seemed like a good idea at the time. What was I thinking?")

One of the keys to the above examples is how important the visual impression is to the making of holistic decisions. Pictures speak more than a thousand words. Of course pictures are also a possible starting point for logical discussion, consideration, and judgment. But when seeing a scene for the first time, it is hard not to react with a quick judgment, which may or may not be followed up with a contemplative reflection of what is truly within the picture.

There is a debate within the animal rights/welfare movement as to which part of the brain should be addressed to get people's attention and change their habits concerning animal treatment. Some use shock images to get the attention of their audience. Others choose to engage in rational, logical discussions. The development of public policy and new laws does and will require considerable use of the logical approach to an issue before the end result can be realized, but arousing the emotion of the public may be a necessary first step toward achieving political action. However, walking into an elected official's office with pictures of bad things happening to animals will usually not produce the desired outcome, even though, as with the downer cattle video, sometimes the dramatic impact of a picture is necessary. Are the pictures of hens in battery cages sufficient for individuals to stop buying eggs from such a facility (assuming they even know that their eggs come from such a place—we buy eggs from the grocery store, not directly from the egg producer)? Perhaps some people would be persuaded, but probably not many. It is hard to know how many people have actually seen videos of battery caged hens and have chosen to not act, compared to individuals who have not seen any such videos.

Returning to the zoo issue, note that it is not like the blood and violence in the clubbing of the baby seal, or the possible intense pain and suffering of Homer's dog, Rover. The visual is not as important or as immediate. As we pass by the cages, we see passive animals, sitting, pacing, or sleeping; there is no blood, no threat of death, and nothing triggers immediate concern in the visitor of something being wrong. But, have the visitors asked the right questions? Do we have sufficient information? As an autistic person who is also a professor of animal welfare, Temple Grandin has a book that makes clear, our information about animal behavior is often seriously lacking, and without this information rational decision-making is truly handicapped.[3]

If the context of respectful use is kept as a frame of reference, then there is a starting point. For the example fact pattern of the zoo, the first question would be: *Is it possible to respect the physical and emotional needs of an animal of a particular species in the spaces that are available in a par-*

ticular zoo? Animals that are known to range widely in the natural environment, such as lions and wolves, may have emotional difficulties living in a cage that allows them to move only 100 feet in any direction. (But what about a specially constructed lion enclosure that mimics the wild?) Penguins will need cold, hummingbirds need warmth. Could any facility accommodate their needs in a respectful way? If not, then they should not be allowed to keep the animals. Some zoos have decided that they cannot accommodate the needs of elephants and have sent the animals to sanctuaries to live out their lives.

At the moment, no law really raises these questions fully. The Federal Animal Welfare Act does require zoos to have certain minimum physical standards, but they are not based upon the emotional and psychological needs of the animals in question, and the law only covers mammals (not reptiles, birds, and other species). These are ethical (and sometimes political) decisions for those who control and direct the zoos around the country and around the world. Self-regulation of the zoos through membership in a private organization like the Association of Zoos and Aquariums does seek a more comprehensive view of the keeping of animals in captivity.[4] But voluntary, private associations are no better in the care of individual animals than the ethics and resources of the individuals that comprise the association. Members of the public can agree or disagree with a particular organization and bring financial and political pressure on the organization to move it to obtain better outcomes for the animals. Can or should we leave it to the experts at the zoos to meet these requirements, or should we draft a more comprehensive law to create specific standards of respectful use? What is the risk that money issues will overcome the respectful use needs of animals in this community?

IMPACT OF MONEY

One great difficulty when making ethical decisions about animals arises when money/profit is part of the context. Is it ethical for the owner and keeper of a horse to take it for a run around the track? Can it be done respectfully? Yes indeed, it is very believable that many horses would like the experience; just as some humans enjoy the physical activity of running at various distances. The key is that the human respects the horse, by understanding what the horse is capable of doing and not asking that it do more. If there is no money at issue, there is much less reason to believe an owner would not be respectful of the horse.

What happens when we add to this picture the impact of money and the physical disassociation of the owners from the horse? Is commercial horse racing ethical? To the degree that outcomes are unethical, for example, the use of illegal drugs and/or racing a horse when it is injured, should horse racing be illegal? It is no longer, if it ever was, solely an athletic event. It is about big money and big egos: money to be spent, money to be gambled, and prize money to be made on the track as well as breeding fees when a horse's racing days are over. The winners are few but wealthy, and the losers lose money. At least some of these humans lose sight of the fact that a horse is a being with limitations as well as abilities, and not just a machine for making money that can be tossed aside if it does not perform. The most obvious evidence of something being wrong is the number of times a horse has been shot and killed on a racetrack because it has broken a leg or is otherwise severely injured while running a race. The risk of racehorses being misused is particularly high when the owner of the horse makes no effort to understand and appreciate his horse. This may arise when the horse is seen not as an individual living being but as an investment. Social judgment about unethical outcomes that occur in the greyhound dog-racing industry has already shut down these racetracks in a number of states.[5]

Consider a horse named Shirley that had great genes, suggesting that she could be a winning racehorse. A group of ten people purchase the horse for $100,000 and turn her over to a trainer to get ready for racing. The trainer makes good money due to his reputation for producing winners. How much will he push the horse to do physical things that put the horse at risk of harm? How often will a trainer or a veterinarian give drugs to the horse to mask the risk of harm in running a race? I don't know the percent, but clearly disrespectful decisions are made, and horses pay the price with their lives and health. Because it keeps happening, it is clear that some owners find it an acceptable risk, so the question is whether we, the public, think these risks to horses are acceptable. Do we need to supersede these individual judgments and assure respectful use with legal action?

This is a judgment that is both holistic and rational. There is no knowable advantage to a horse in assuming this kind of risk. The advantage is only to the horse's owners who seek to gain money, reputation, and ego stroking. Those do not seem particularly important to me. So my personal judgment is that unless the industry can reduce the risk of harm to horses to near zero, then the activity should be banned. Let the rich play with their other toys but not living beings. What is your judgment? What factors do you believe to be important here?

What if we change the context for horse racing so that the primary motive for disrespecting the horse will be eliminated? What if a law was passed that said the maximum winning pot for any horse race was $10,000, and 10 percent of every dollar won by a horse had to be set aside in a trust for the future benefit of that horse? Would that be enough of a buffer against the corruption of money to ensure respectful use?

> The purpose of life is not to make money.
> We make money in order to seek the purpose of life.

INFORMATION

Let us focus for a minute on how dependent good ethical judgments are on having good information. A premise of respectful use is that the possessor of an animal has an obligation by virtue of his or her intimate connection to the animal to seek out information about that animal in order to make respectful judgments about how to act toward and support the animal. Consider a fifty-year-old woman named Charlotte who has had a financially successful life in marketing children's clothing but wants to pursue another direction. Being tired of the big-city grind, she contemplates moving to the countryside and raising sheep because she thinks there is an upscale urban market for cheese made from sheep's milk. Her plan is to buy a farm, get fifty ewes and five rams, and start marketing her sheep cheese in the big city. At the moment, there is nothing to stop her from doing so if she has the money. But she is clueless as to what is important for the health and well-being of the sheep.

An ethical seller of sheep would not sell to her unless the person was satisfied that she has the resources and the requisite information to support the sheep appropriately. Is there adequate fenced acreage with existing pasture, or at least access to quality hay? Is there a barn and water supply? Does she have a veterinarian? Are there predator risks in her area? Does she know about supplemental minerals she may need to give the sheep to compensate for any deficiencies in the food source from the local environment? Does she know about sheering the sheep, and who will do it? Does she know about likely parasites, and does she have a control program in mind? Does she understand the shots that newborn sheep require? Does she know anything about birthing lambs? Does she know about the factors that will be important in setting breeding groups? The information necessary to raise sheep respectfully is significant. And if she bought that number of sheep to start with, there is a real risk that she could be overwhelmed on the learning curve. If she does not have an agricultural animal background, it will take considerable time to "see" the sheep, so that there can be awareness of possible problems with individuals in the flock. (A flock of sheep needs to be observed over a considerable time period in order to establish what is normal conduct and activity for the flock and the individuals within the flock before being able to discern in a timely manner when the pattern is being broken and whether one or more individual sheep are at a health risk.)

Before the life and welfare of so many beings are put at risk, she needs information, which can only grow with experience into knowledge. The particularly difficult part is that she may in good faith not even understand what questions to ask, let alone the likely answers. Again, one would hope that a respectful seller of sheep would provide this information as well as offer support and coaching after the sheep are delivered. But if the seller does not care and the buyer is ignorant, then the risk that the sheep could suffer and die is high. Perhaps society has to step in and say, "You need to take a class and do site visits of existing sheep operations before you can take delivery of the sheep." Much like requiring a driver's license before you can drive, there should be a sheep-knowledge test that you must pass before you can possess and raise sheep—just a thought to put on the table.

Should we require an education test before a dog is brought into the home? Information is critical if we are to make respectful-use decisions. The question becomes, How do we make sure the information is obtained by the individuals who will make the animal-use decisions?

WEIGHING THE INTERESTS

In the above examples when a rational, thoughtful judgment is made, there normally is a weighing of competing interests. The outcome of the thought process in deciding whether or not to do something will be a result of weighing the benefits and costs of the action or inaction to all of the relevant ethical subjects; that is what makes something an ethical question.

RESPECTING ANIMALS

The immediate difficulty is finding the correct currency to use in doing the weighing. What are the marks on the scale? We all understand money and understand (sort of) how to calculate the financial benefits and costs of an action or inaction. But, as suggested in the previous chapter, ethical decisions must often take into account other values. Our public policy accepts the importance of other values, but it is often impossible to put numbers, let alone dollar amounts, on these values. Many people believe in the value of preserving and restoring endangered species; consider the government efforts in supporting the restoration of the eagle and the wolf in the United States. We believe (or at least express the belief) that families should be supported as the key social group from which societies emerge. We also believe that children should not be abused.

Is it ethical to keep lions or elephants in a big public zoo? What are the benefits and the costs to the humans and to the animals that will inhabit the zoo? The human organization that controls the zoo will be the owner of the animals and make the critical decisions about their well-being and care. The humans might perceive two interests being served by having mega fauna on the premises: First, it will help draw customers who will pay the entrance fee or become supporting members of the zoo. It can be presumed that economic success is a base premise in their decision-making. Second, the human organization may well see such ownership and displays as partial fulfillment of their corporate mission to provide the public with positive animal interactive experiences. As discussed in the first chapter, this can be complex and not so easily monetized. What is the social and environmental value of a zoo exhibit containing lions and elephants that results in a dozen individuals deciding to dedicate their lives to protecting lions and elephants in their natural habitat? What is the value of a pleasant day at the zoo for a thousand humans? It is more than the cost of admission, but again, it is hard to calculate.

If you see some difficulties in measuring the human benefits, consider what might happen when you attempt to value the consequences to the individual animals. For this purpose, we can accept as a premise that basic food and veterinary care will be available. Do we have the information necessary to make a judgment about the consequences to the individual animals at a particular zoo? What will be their quality of life—as measured by what? This book is not the place for the factual resolution of the questions I am raising. But assuming that you can reach some judgment about quality of life for the animals, what value is put upon that and how is it weighed against the human benefits? We seek a rational judgment about an ethical question, but the reality is that for most of us it can be a lengthy and only somewhat (but never really fully) informed holistic one.

THE ETHICS OF PURCHASING

We humans make purchases every day, from things as simple as a cup of coffee to a $4,000 carving made from the ivory of an elephant tusk. Each purchase ought to be considered an ethical decision, but seldom are they considered as such. When we spend money, we create a market preference for a particular activity or commodity. The invisible hand of the market will engage the capitalist system to provide you with the item that you want, be it in a lawful market or a black market. If you want a cup of coffee, someone has to grow the beans, harvest the beans, roast the beans, and then package and ship the beans to you. The purchaser of the cup of coffee has no idea who has performed these tasks, or at what cost to the growers or to the environment. Over a decade ago, consumers in the developed world came to understand that humans who grew the coffee beans often did not seem to be appropriately paid for their efforts; instead, others in the chain of commerce made the larger profits. To deal with this problem the concept of fair-trade coffee was developed.[6]

Your rich cup of fair-trade coffee can help farmers escape poverty. Most small-scale family coffee growers live in remote locations and lack access to credit, so they are vulnerable to middlemen who offer cash for their coffee beans at a fraction of its value. Fair trade guarantees farmers a minimum price and links farmers directly with importers, creating long-term sustainability. Through fair trade, farmers earn better incomes, allowing them to hold on to their land and invest in quality crops.[7]

Then the consumers of coffee received the information that considerable wildlife habitat was being destroyed to make room for the coffee plantations. But this did not seem right or fair to the wildlife that die and whose habitat is lost in order for consumers to have a cup of coffee in the morning. So the Smithsonian Institute's Migratory Bird Center started a project promoting coexistence between commercial coffee plants and wildlife by urging that coffee plants be planted in the shade of existing natural plants.[8]

These are examples of the most abstract type of ethical decisions. The humans or wildlife whose existence is impacted by the decision of a consumer to buy coffee will not have been within the immediate awareness of the coffee drinker; indeed, it is usually impossible to even ask about whose existence is impacted. This is because coffee is an international commodity, thus it difficult to determine the specific individuals involved. But not knowing where the consequences occur or on whom they fall does not mean there are no consequences. This is an ethical decision within the context of the global community that we share with other humans and wildlife. While our duty may be light, it is still present.

Of course the first level of difficulty is creating the awareness in the consumers of coffee that their actions have an impact on other beings, and that therefore purchasing a cup of coffee is an action with ethical consequences. The second problem is obtaining information that allows for a good decision to be made. Because that information is basically impossible to obtain at the point of purchase of that cup of coffee, frustration arises for those who are willing to make an ethical decision. The concept of providing symbols on consumer goods, such as the fair-trade symbols, has been one such cultural answer to this problem. The consumer delegates the information gathering and weighing of interests (e.g., what is a fair price to pay the growers of coffee) to an organization that communicates the presence of an acceptable balance of interests through the symbol on the consumer packaging. This is an appropriate way to deal with the light ethical issue that the purchase of coffee represents.

Let's look at the second purchase mentioned above: The ivory carving is different. the carving itself is valuable because it is ivory and not a plastic substitute. Ivory comes from elephant tusks. To consider buying it is an ethical and legal decision. It is a legal issue because, with only a very few exceptions, it is illegal to import ivory under the US Endangered Species Act, and it is illegal to kill the elephant in its natural habitat, based upon local statutes of the countries involved. Purchasing the carving is an ethical issue because in today's world the brutal, premature death of a specific elephant is required to obtain the raw ivory. (There are no humane slaughterhouses for elephants.) Whether or not the human carvers of the ivory are paid appropriately for their service is another ethical concern, but I do not know and choose to set aside this issue in the face of the death of the elephant. Killing elephants in general will have ecological consequences at some level, but more immediate is the death of the elephant herself and the consequences to the social group of which that elephant was a member. This is the killing not of insects but of intelligent beings that deserve a high level of respect within the community of global wildlife. In no ethical world is the death of the elephant justified by the human "need" to purchase ivory objects. Finally, there is the additional value of protecting an endangered species.

What would be the benefit to the purchaser of the ivory carving? Enjoyment of the visual and tactile feel of the carving might indeed be a positive for that person. Perhaps it is a simple financial investment, in which the purchaser believes the carving will increase in value over time, or for perceived health benefits.[9] But there are many alternatives available to the purchaser for these motives. Many who can afford the cost of such an item are, in all likelihood, aware of the illegality of the purchase and the death of an unseen elephant to provide the ivory. Often the purchase of the item suggests an assertion of human ego, of showing that purchaser's importance within the human communities that he or she inhabits. It is unlikely that you or I would change the mind of such a person with additional information or a well-crafted rational argument. Is the answer more information, more law, or changing the habits and beliefs within some human communities? So long as the consumer demand exists, the elephant deaths will continue.

Ethical judgments occur every day, when dealing both with the animals in front of us and the animals around the world, unseen and unidentified, but impacted by global trade.

CHAPTER 13

WE ARE THE GODS OF OLD

In room A we have a man, standing naked, looking out the window. In room B we have a chimpanzee, standing naked, looking out the window. What do we see? How are they alike and how do they differ? Their biology and DNA are very similar. Both will act to avoid pain and request of you (in their own way) not to inflict it. This gives an ethical presumption to both, as ethical subjects, that I should not impose pain upon them without a very good cause.

The man is both an ethical actor and an ethical subject. The chimpanzee, on the other hand, is primarily an ethical subject; the chimpanzee is an ethical actor only in the modest way that a very young child is when learning to deal with others. Let's examine the differences between the man and the chimpanzee. The man designed the software for a computer system that the chimpanzee might be able to use at a rudimentary level but could never design. Two thousand years ago, the humans of the time would have considered the computer a miracle or a demon. The man can arrange for a new habitat to be built for the chimpanzee, but the chimpanzee cannot do the same for the man. The man can have the natural habitat of the chimpanzee clear-cut and sold to assorted lumber companies; not only can the chimpanzee do nothing about it, the chimpanzee may well die because of such an action. The man has information and powers many orders of magnitude greater than the chimpanzee.

Now plug in a dog, a crow, and or a snake into the above paragraphs, and the difference is even more stark. Don't even try with a jellyfish.

Note that this chapter's title suggests a multiplicity of gods. I do not seek to engage anyone's religious beliefs, and I do not claim for humans any vision or wisdom that is godlike. Rather, the chapter title suggests that a higher level of control and impact on the beings and physical processes of this earth is now within the conscious and unconscious control of humans, both as individuals and when organized as states and corporations. Human activity now has effects that in the past could have been attributed only to one's god(s). Perhaps it is best to think of us as the gods of ancient Greece and Rome: they were claimed to be all too human in emotions and limited in wisdom, but with powers not previously available to mortals.

We have given ourselves exceptional physical capacities, yet those human traits that have supported our advancement into this new evolutionary position may not be adequate to exercise the judgment required to ensure the respectful use of the beings of this planet. This is about the community of all beings. Our highest level of abstraction contains our most difficult issues about ethical duties toward others. Frankly, the question is, Are we respectfully using our planet and the inhabitants therein?

HOW HAS THIS HAPPENED?

How have we become godlike? First our evolution gave us a language center in our brain with amazing flexibility, capable of understanding and producing all of the languages of the planet. Next came the critical step that no other animal has been able to take, to transfer information from within the brain to external storage devices: from stone tablets, to parchments and books, and now, something that humans of only a one hundred years ago clearly would believe an act of the gods, little thumb drives with unthinkable storage capacity for information. (The early science fiction writer Jules Verne might be the sole exception.)

We humans can accumulate our knowledge; with every other animal, unless they have taught their offspring, the knowledge they learn through life disappears when they die. They have no way of recording their knowledge. Our information, the trivial and the profound, can be recorded and saved indefinitely. Just as the printing press made this stored information available to a much wider circle of humans, our digital world and Internet search engines make most of human knowledge and digital information just finger strokes away. Wisdom is a lot harder to find, but I am sure it must be there.

Historically, as the information accumulated, individual humans discovered new information and developed new technology. At first it was simple things to aid humans in their activities. But at some point, perhaps at the time gun powder was discovered, but certainly by the discovery of nuclear power, the power dynamic between species changed entirely. We had what no other animal had: the ability to transform power beyond what the individual could do. The bow and arrow was an aid to individual humans, as was the flintlock rifle. But how do these compare to a nuclear aircraft carrier with fifty planes and a pile of cruise missiles? Every other animal is limited in its physical impact on the natural world to that which it can do with its own physical abilities. At the same time that the knowledge and power of the individual human is accelerating, the number of humans has increased dramatically. In any time frame relevant to ecosystems and evolution, the level of seven billion humans (and counting) represents extraordinary positive and negative risks for all of the other species. Will this power be used respectfully?

We humans today have godlike capacities beyond the imagination of our early ancestors. Not only do we know about the speed of light and the power of gravity, we can also see the viruses around us and in us. Indeed, we humans in a collective sense now possess the power of life. Genetic engineering is a reality. We can make life that has never existed in the natural world. This door of human knowledge has just been opened. What will be possible in a hundred years? What did the Wright brothers think possible about human flight a hundred years ago compared to where we are today? The future is not always foreseeable, because we are always limited by the knowledge we currently possess.

RESPECTING ANIMALS

It has been a breathtaking run from when humans gathered around a social fire in the woods to putting humans in a space station orbiting around Earth. We are not animals in the definition of evolution; we have long since pushed ourselves to the status of mini-gods relative to other species on the planet. Of course the information and power is not uniformly distributed among all humans. During the twentieth century there was a wide disparity among humans who could take advantage of our information and power. Over the past ten years or so the benefits of being the information species has spread dramatically with the ubiquitous use of cell-phone technology, a tool that has the capacity to swiftly overcome limitations of individual isolation and provide information access for many billions of humans (a study conducted by the United Nations suggests that six billion humans have access to cell phones[1]), drawing our communities closer together.

In today's world of the super-empowered individual, some humans have personal wealth in the billions of dollars. This wealth combined with political and social connections support their capacity to do extraordinary things, both positive and negative, each having ethical impacts on both other humans and other beings. Bill Gates and his foundation can take on the issue of overcoming human death by malaria. Or one unidentified person can post pictures of the brutal beheading executions of Americans on the Internet for millions to see.

HUMANS AS THE INFORMATION SPECIES

Our human community is the first of the information species on this planet. Historically, biological species are driven by the unseen hand of evolution. The environments in which biological species exist shape the evolution of the species. For more than a century, we humans have had the power to reshape the environment in which we live to our liking. We have the capacity to control the environment and in so doing frustrate the unseen hand of evolution. We are just on the threshold of having the capacity to intentionally and directly change our own DNA. Some individuals object to such exercises of power, suggesting that it is wrong to play god. But we are the gods. It is going to happen. The question is, Who will direct it and toward what ends?

Beyond ourselves, we now have the capacity to control and destroy, or direct and support life on this earth. To morally or legally equate a dog to a child is to miss the context of humans as members of this new type of species. It is not so much that this means that the individual human has a higher ethical value than the individual dog. Rather, it means that we have the burden of figuring out how and when to use our power and information, because with great power comes great responsibility.

Pause for a minute before your ego expands to fill the room; recognize that the transformation of humans into the information species is very recent, and it is not at all clear that this is a stable state of affairs. There are a number of paths forward in time that eventually bring humans to a place in which we lose our information advantage and quickly revert to a traditional biological species. Retention of this new status is not assured, and given the present state of the world, politically and ecologically, the status can be considered very fragile indeed. In time, admittedly several billion years from now, our own sun might put an end to our lofty status with one big solar flare that fries all information receptacles in the world. But I think human actions and inactions are the highest risk to our continued existence as the information species. Do we have the wisdom and political will to control the power that we possess? The following memos suggest that all the information we have may or may not be sufficient to control the future of ourselves or the other living beings of our planet. Our broadest ethical duty, to preserve and promote the life of humans and animals, may not be realized.

RESPECTING ANIMALS

PROFESSOR XYBERY LECTURE

Occasional Very Short Stories Series

Lectures by Nonhuman Beings about Human Beings
By: Professor Xybery (Date: 022.555.23933) (Universe 223)
University of Liddum, Ramatus
Course 408, Species Directed Self-Evolution into Stability, Lecture 17

Version #1

Today we shall focus our attention on the most critical step in the evolution of a species into thinking beings, the Barrium Threshold (BT). Those of us who have reached the stability of post-Barrium evolution can only marvel that our genetic ancestors had the balance and wisdom to make it through that difficult transformation. As we have noted before, the process of biological evolution is very straightforward, regardless of time or location in the galaxy. Your basic courses in biology, genetics, and ecology have provided you with these universal rules. As you will remember, being on the path of increasing intelligence can mean survival for a species. Intelligence can provide the necessary edge for survival, but other attributes are also genetically successful. It is usually the case on a planet that after the evolution of movable life on land, it is only a billion or so years before some species will obtain an edge by evolving intelligence. While this process may be slow, building for a time, when the language creation barrier is broken, the Evivan Threshold, then things can develop at an ever-accelerating pace. In perhaps as little as a hundred thousand years after the species develops language, there comes the accumulation of knowledge and the discovery of tools and technology that support the gaining of more knowledge and brings the species to the Barrium Threshold.

Our work over the past century on the planet known to the prior inhabitants as Earth has provided us with an excellent example of a species unable to pass through the Barrium Threshold. It occurred during their designated time of the twenty-first century, or approximately 033.988.13060 on our calendar.

Let us remind ourselves that the Barrium Threshold is that point at which a species becomes self-aware of the genetic code upon which their lives are built, allowing them to manipulate and create beings, while at the same time the nonintellectual characteristics of the species are pushing the species toward self-destruction. Characteristics such as greed, pride, self-promotion, a focus upon the immediate and visible, and constant sexual reproduction, which were all important in pushing the species toward the BT, will bring it down if not controlled. Thus, the BT is successfully passed through when the power of genetics is used to reduce or control the negative characteristics of the species. The effect of the change is to place the species in harmony with the other live beings on the planet.

Inherent in the gaining of the knowledge that places a species at the BT is the raising of ethical questions about how to treat other genetically driven beings and the new beings that the species is able to create. Whether this ethical issue is fully addressed is usually predictive of whether the species passes through the BT. It is the ethical questions that ought to drive the species to use the genetic information to seek new solutions. On Earth, their twenty-first century saw the collapse of the human species (*Homo sapiens sapiens*). And it was fifty thousand years before the dolphins were able to rise up and pass through the Barrium Threshold and join the other successful races of the galaxy.

Consider the Classic Issues Faced by Humans

Excessive sexual reproduction resulted in the species spreading out over all the available landmasses, reducing the genetic diversity of the planet by the killing off of competing species. Amazingly, they allowed all of the other primates of their evolutionary family to go extinct. While the killing off of competitors is natural in mindless evolution, the lack of ethical concern for other beings suggests the species' intelligence was unable to control individual conduct.

The demand for immediate profit and protein resulted in the ecological collapse of the world's fisheries. This was one of the triggers of the species' collapse.

While the appropriate ethical issues were raised and discussed by portions of their society, the economically powerful controlled the political process, making the implementation of new ethical perspectives almost impossible.

The individual drive of some humans for wealth, ego gratification, and selfish wishes resulted in poor allocation of resources, great bitterness, and division between the members of the species. This division resulted in wars between the resource-rich and those without, and between have-nots who wanted to climb over each other to become rich.

Like adolescents with new toys, humans created and destroyed without any awareness of the respect for life necessary to move to the next level of evolution.

Politically, the issue of national sovereignty was allowed to trump all other values, allowing the selfish, narrow interests of some states to inflict global consequences upon all.

Their planet-wide movement of goods and people driven by global capitalism resulted in the translocation of species into new environments, exotic species causing conflicts with long-existing local species. Only the most ruthless and aggressive species survived, resulting in the dangerous simplification of ecosystems around the world.

Moving into the realm of the use of genetic information, with the primary force of global capitalism at work, genetically modified animals and plants were shipped around the world, ignoring the safety and stability provided by natural genetic diversity. Again, these acts were signs of an egotistical unawareness, or worse, a lack of concern about predictable ecological consequences.

The presence of a global industrial animal protein system resulted in local human populations being unable to provide for themselves. They had relied entirely on megacorporations to deliver food from great distances away; this was very economically efficient, but high-risk.

Foreseeable climate change arose as a result of an increasing population with increasing per capita energy consumption, again resulting in loss of species and the inability to protect ecological complexity.

While cases of species failure differ in the details of the collapse, the general pattern is clear. A calamity will occur that brings global transportation to a halt, resulting in the starvation of millions of individuals who had relied upon global food distribution for their survival. This is the predictable result of unchecked free trade in food that moves from local to global corporate control. The threads of the economy that were part of the global reach come apart. Unemployment surges, tax collection drops, government spending becomes inflationary, and millions lose their jobs. The final step is when the global communication system breaks down and individuals of the species must return to a state of locally based resources for survival, instead of their globally based resource-distribution system. Fairly quickly, death occurs for those unable to support their lives locally, resulting in a large population collapse as the rules of ecology ruthlessly reassert themselves, as in the case of any species that expands beyond the carrying capacity of the environment in which it lives.

In the case of humans on Earth, the collapse occurred during their years of 2033–2035. A number of different events occurred in a short period of time. Political instability in the Middle East resulted in one party using a nuclear weapon against another, which in turn resulted in countermeasures that resulted in much death, but, more importantly, sharply slowed the production of fossil-based hydrocarbons. A virus was found in South American cattle that put consumers at risk. The response was to shut down imports of the beef, but there were inadequate supplies in much of the world and a glut at other locations. A drought in the western United States, in Canada, and in Russia reduced wheat and corn production. The United States and other countries were spending so much money on building dikes around their major cities to stop the sea rise that inflation took hold of the dollar and investors got spooked and withdrew billions from the US stock and bond markets. Gold became very expensive.

Business began to fail and hunger arrived in the major cities, resulting in political unrest, and an attitude of protectionism on the local level took precedence over global interests. This had a downward spiraling effect with the resulting loss of more jobs and a significant increase in violence. In the United States there were almost no factories left, and it took only a few mad individuals to stop the flow of energy pipelines within the country. Members of the middle class could not pay their bills; the dollar was not worth much; the large corporations ground to a halt, laying off even more people. The state tried to take over communication, but local control points had long since been phased out in the name of corporate efficiency, and rebuilding them in a short period of time was impossible. While the United States and China had to address serious internal matters, the rest of the world started local wars over water and wheat, causing resource shortages, and again creating political instability and investor nervousness. Someone cut the communication into and out of three of the major stock exchanges, and the global economy came to a halt. The movement of people out of cities, where no food existed, into the countryside, produced local violence, as the countryside could absorb only a few of the city dwellers. Might became right, and law was at the end of a gun, until they ran out of ammunition. Intellectual and cultural activities, such as universities, had no paying students and had to shut down.

The global village was returned to local villages; the global flow of money and investments reverted to a barter system. Animal protein was not available in many areas. When the genetically created food animals were taken out of their industrial confinement, they were unable to survive in an open-air, grass-based system, as they had existed when humans were a developing species. The human population quickly killed off all the local wildlife that might have been a food source. Previously, grain crops had been genetically modified by large corporations so that the seeds could grow for only one generation; then it was necessary to buy more seeds from them the next year. When the corporations collapsed, the seeds were no longer available. Most areas had no backup seed stock, so large-scale grain farming failed. Whereas in the past humans had been able to subsist off local fisheries and wildlife, these resources had all been destroyed in the years leading up to the current conflict. There was almost nothing to eat for billions of people. Humans simply starved, and they did not go quietly. In the process of their collapse, humans stripped areas of anything editable, leaving a destroyed ecosystem in many places that would take thousands of years to reestablish balance and complexity.

Within a brief two years, the species lost all but the most primitive of technology. Their population was only 15 percent of its previous numbers, and most of these were humans who had previously existed in local economies disconnected from the previous global economy.

Or perhaps in ten thousand years the efforts by humans to find the positive path forward will be acknowledged by the professor.

Occasional Very Short Stories Series

Future Lectures from Nonhuman Beings about Human Beings
By: Professor Xybery (Date: 022.555.23933) (Universe 224)
University of Liddum, Ramatus
Course 408, Species Directed Self-Evolution into Stability, Lecture #17

Version #2

On Earth the twenty-first-century humans reached the tipping point, and while it was touch-and-go for a while, they were able to work through the maze of technology and political decisions.

The key point was when it was realized that additional intelligence, vision, and self-control were going to be a necessity, or human activity would not get past the Barrium Threshold (our name, not theirs). Next it was realized that the necessity of changing human beings was not going to happen by evolution; the process was too slow and not manageable because of the billions of beings that existed. Therefore, the logical next step was to enhance the existing brains of as many humans as possible. While different species have addressed the same issue with different approaches, the humans chose brain enhancement during the age of two to twenty-one years as the primary method. Using information derived from stem-cell research, and nano-technology for delivery, medical personnel delivered molecules into the neocortex of an individual's brain. After ten years of treatment, the neocortex and frontal lobe in particular had 10 percent more neurons within that portion and 30 percent more connections between the frontal lobe and the locomotion and speech centers. "Enhanced intelligence" was defined as the ability to see and comprehend patterns plus the ability to control and direct behaviors toward long-range goals, with a dampening of emotions and impulses. Among other results, this treatment counteracted the genius effect, which often caused those of high intellectual capacity not to work well in political or social contexts.

Of course it should be noted that humans almost did not make the transition, as there was a strong movement against enhanced humans, but ultimately the enhanced humans got control of the political process and withstood the wave of opposition. The tipping point came when about 10 percent of the population in the developed countries over the age of twenty-five had received the treatment at some point in their lives.

The usual unexpected consequences included the elimination of boxing as a sport, creation of exceptional gardens in all parts of the world, and the equivalent of three Beethovens and five Einsteins within a forty-year period.

At first it was only suggested that elected offices should be reserved for the enhanced adults, but after a decade many countries required that all elected officials worldwide be enhanced. What was essential to the transformation, but not foreseeable by many who took the treatment in order to enhance power and wealth, was that after the treatment they came to understand how limited such goals were and how humans needed a longer, broader vision.

As has been shown by repeated studies, that 90 percent of the species that make it past the Barrium Threshold do so only by developing group self-awareness as a significant limitation on individual self-awareness. Genetic evolution inherently pushes toward self-awareness as a significant positive factor for survival. This allows for self-preservation and self-protection to become clearer goals and allows for a long-term focus on activities. While this phase will also produce some degree of empathy and altruism, selfish self-fulfillment is the dominant motivation for action or inaction. It becomes nearly impossible to make political decisions for the benefit of those controlling the political system or future generations. Usually a capitalist economic system becomes dominant because it so clearly allows self-interests to effectively and efficiently make short-term decisions. But to save a species (and the supporting ecosystem) from self-destruction requires a next step, in which individual actions are tempered by awareness of consequences of the actions upon others tied with an actual concern for the welfare of others. (The Vulcans remain a prime example for the positive path forward.) When this occurs, the simplistic and negative outcomes of capitalism are realized and a post-capitalism period occurs during which business decisions are still separate from political decisions, but more non-economic values are imposed upon the process. Before these events, such ideas might have been clustered under the title "socialism," but this attitude came to be known as "humanized capitalism."

Several genetic paths are available for this phase, including hive awareness, but usually it is obtained by significant enhancement in intelligence, as reflected in pattern identification and abstractness that result in a much broader awareness of impacts of actions on others. Additionally, there is a significant broadening of the communities of which each individual considers himself or herself a part. A typical side effect is the specific inclusion of other species in their community, which in turn becomes a motivation for better care and respect for the needs of other species. While this process is not necessarily aimed at reduction of volatile emotional reactions, it is a common side effect, such that while all prior emotions still exist and can operate, they are less triggered by self-protection and ego gratification and more by fulfilling the needs and reducing the suffering of others.

THE DUTIES OF THE GODS

As we sit high on our imaginary Mount Olympus, surveying the contradictory activities of billions of humans, how do we organize our thoughts? How might we show our respect for others at such high levels of abstraction, where the individual melds into ecosystem identification?

The starting point should be, again, respect for others; respect for the millions of biological species from which we have tentatively separated. Also, there needs to be a humbleness about the power we possess—awareness of the consequences of the exercise of power on other beings, as well as on ourselves. It is useful to break the issues into two broad categories: those within us and those outside of us. Outside of us is the physical world in which we live, the communities that we share with other humans and other beings. Within us is the unseen world of our DNA.

The following are the results of decades of pondering any number of issues. A broader dialogue with many others may well result in modifying these premises of perspective. It is a result of my holistic judgment.

1. **Premise about the habitats for all beings on Earth:** Human activity should seek diversity of life and a higher density of life within that diversity. Given the proven human capacity for eco-

system destruction, we must go beyond the idea of preservation of the environment by:

    a. supporting existing systems so as to retain ecological viability,
    b. preserving natural areas not yet impacted by human activity,
    c. adopting positive programs to recover degraded ecosystems,
    d. creating new ecosystems, in particular to make up for the destruction of prior ecosystems.

2. **Premise for the individuals within the ecosystems:** We should promote opportunities that allow individual beings to realize and to experience those capacities that their DNA has provided them.

BEING A CIVITIST

The duty to other beings requires us first to ensure they have a place to live, to exist. This duty is also broader and deeper than that which is usually incorporated within the term "environmentalism." Therefore, a new term will be used to describe an individual who accepts the duties set out above: a "civitist."

Supporting, preserving, and protecting existing habitats is within the realm of a normal environmental focus. We in the United States have an extensive system of ecological protections with our parks and national forest and reserves. But in many parts of the world, even when important wildlife areas have been identified, they have not received the requisite protections. As 2018 begins, we continue to see the protected lands of the United States put at risk under the policies of President Donald Trump.[2]

Restoration is difficult and expensive. We may or may not understand what is critical to reboot an environmentally degraded area. If a farmer decided to leave a field alone so that the natural prairie can be restored, it most likely will not work, at least not on a timescale meaningful to humans. An ecosystem is a dynamic place where the interactions of both plants and animals create a pattern of life and death within the capacity of the place.

RESPECTING ANIMALS

Most prairie ecosystems require the presence of grazing animals and the actions of fire to maintain a specific diversity of life. An unused cornfield will just become a weed field with the most aggressive alien species taking over; this will normally not support a good diversity of wildlife.

Of course some issues are very difficult to approach. If we do not wish to degrade the near-shore ecosystem of the Gulf of Mexico every summer, some method of controlling the flow of agricultural runoff contained in the Mississippi River must be developed. To preserve the ecosystems of the western rivers, the human consumption of water must be reduced or contained. The laws of the western states concerning freshwater resources reflect the mentality of the times when the west was originally settled, not the present day. But of course the value of water has created a significant vested interest in continuing with old rules, to the detriment of existing wildlife and the habitat they need to live. Then again, the twenty- or thirty-year effects of global warming, another negative human impact on the life of the planet, may negate any difference that changing the legal system might obtain. There simply will not be enough water for present human use. I suspect that the burden will first fall on the wildlife.

To intentionally create a desert out of a forest, field, or prairie would be seen by everyone as a sad waste for both humans and wildlife. A place of no or little life is a negative state of affairs. Yet humans intentionally support a near desert-like environmental status when they support mono-cultures in agriculture and forestry. Chemical farmers are the opposite of civitist. They seek to destroy and kill anything that is not their crop. They support no diversity of life and will kill the diversity of life when they begin farming an area. There is no concern for the health and well-being of the soil; therefore, the existence or well-being of the diversity of life is not just ignored, but intentionally destroyed. A field of corn may have considerable biomass per square foot, but it has no biodiversity. While this may provide maximum profit for some humans, it represents a failure of our ethical duty to other beings of this planet. It is the ultimate conflict in values, where the weight of the lives and well-being of thousands of small, perhaps unseen creatures mean nothing when weighted against the profit to the chemical farmer and the megacorporations that support the endeavor.

In the "inefficient" farms of a century ago, there was room for the crops and the wildlife. Indeed, the humans who seek only economic efficiencies are the enemy of the ecological complexities critical to our duty to be a good civitist. A pasture can be full of sheep or cattle while supporting a rich and diverse local habitat for wildlife. A good pasture starts with supporting and developing good soil, the opposite of the mono-crop mentality.

Of course there are many human activities that destroy and degrade local environments: fishing practices, strip-mining, clear-cutting, road building, dam building, pollution dumping, and so on. While many of the most egregious of these activities now occur outside the United States, it is often the consumer demand of the developed world that creates the financial incentives for these destructive activities. The focus on mono-agriculture is because it is perhaps the largest single land use in the United States. We are the gods of destruction and creation.

THE DEER PARK PROBLEM

A concern for protection of ecosystems has often caused a conflict with those who seek to protect the life of individual animals. Animal welfare/rights advocates often oppose the intentional killing of deer in small parks controlled by local or regional governments. While protection of individual life is always a high priority, there are times when individual life must give way to the greater good of the other beings in an area.

Deer populations within confined city or county parks often produce a clear example of this conflict of views. If there are no predators within the human-created and human-controlled park, then there is a risk (almost a certainty) of deer births creating a condition of overpopulation. That is, the number of deer will grow to the point that they exceed the carrying capacity of the park (available food production). Unless the deer population is reduced, the deer will consume the vegetation of the park, killing off all the other grazing species, such as rabbits, as well as the predators that depend on the presence of prey such as rabbits. The deer would also be eliminating the habitat of other species such as ground-nesting birds and frogs.

If a rich and diverse ecosystem is a desired outcome, as all civitists desire, then the number of deer has to be controlled in the absence of natural predators. Often, in the eyes of people who care about local animals, the foreseeable death and suffering of the individual deer is unacceptable. Negative views about sport hunting add to the heat of passion. But it is not a sport-hunting issue. We humans have created an unnatural ecosystem, with a lack of predators to keep the population of herbivores in balance. This results in an imbalance of the ecosystem. In the long run, it will be destructive for the deer themselves; their overpopulation will destroy their food base through overconsumption, and the deer will begin to starve. The ensuing suffering and death will perhaps bring the deer population down to the sustainable levels, but then the cycle will begin again.

We are the gods that created the situation with fences and the death of natural predators; for the balance and well-being of all the living beings within the ecosystem, we must accept the responsibility for ecosystem maintenance. While the introduction of a wolf pack would restore the natural balance, the risk of other negative outcomes might mitigate against such an approach in most places. The deer population should be kept in balance with the ecosystem in which they exist. How to accomplish the balance is a complex issue to be solved on a case-by-case basis. (Perhaps the use of birth control would work, perhaps not.)

Would the story be different if the subject was elephants rather than deer?

INDIVIDUAL LIFE

If the goal of the second premise is that we should promote opportunities that allow individual beings to realize and experience those capacities that their DNA has provided them, then the context for human conduct continues to be that of respectful use as set out in this book. If wildlife exists in a habitat where human activity is not really present, then while there may be a duty of habitat preservation, we have no control, no responsibility for the life experiences of each individual animal. It must be understood that some, perhaps most, individual beings born into that community will have short lives with frightening ends, as they are consumed or harmed by other animals. The laws of evolution and ecosystems proceed as they have for billions of years; we cannot revoke those laws.

If wildlife exists in human-provided enclosures such as zoos and aquariums, then there is a standard by which to decide if the holding of the animal is respectful. Does the enclosure combined with the management practices of the human keepers provide sufficient opportunities for the individual held to experience those capacities that their DNA has provided them? But of course this simple test has great complexities. Should the zoo provide the lion with live gazelle to hunt and kill for dinner? Can the management of the lion separate the lion's need to experience hunting from the need to consume meat? We are the gods who decide who lives and who dies and under what conditions both will happen.

THE DNA WITHIN LIFE

A second major category of individual animals to be concerned about arises out of controlling and manipulating the DNA of life. Now we need to distinguish between the evolution of species and breeds by the natural or human selection of parents who combine their DNA to produce a new generation of life, and the biological science of genetic engineering.

RESPECTING ANIMALS

Humans have been breeding animals since the beginning of the domestication process. It has resulted in Great Danes and Chow Chows being different breeds of the same species. While some of the extreme outcomes of this process can be troubling, that is not the focus of concern here.

Genetic manipulation is important because it represents the possibility of a different community of animals. Species and individuals are not just nudged by selective breeding but are created solely for human use. With this godlike power comes the issue of what community will exist or be created between humans and these animals. Will they be cherished pets or the hidden animals of an agricultural community, living a life of unseen suffering for corporate profit? What will be our ethical duty to these animals? There is a risk that they will be considered different from "natural" animals, with less concern for their well-being as created entities and more for human short-term economic well-being. Manipulation of genes has within it both the power to enhance the quality of life and to degrade the experience of life. Who shall decide or limit such activity?

For example, what if someone manipulated the genes of a chicken so that the bird was constantly hungry and would eat as much as possible, resulting in 50 percent more weight gain per week? The chicken could be slaughtered earlier to reduce overhead costs, thereby enhancing profit. But such a chicken would be under constant stress, driven by an unnatural desire to eat, constantly looking for food, setting aside all other natural movements and activities. The chicken would add weight so fast that its bones and muscles would be inadequate to support it. In the last three weeks of life, the chicken would suffer lameness and joint stress. By the time of slaughtering, the chicken would barely be capable of walking. The reduction in overhead costs would benefit the stockholders of the corporation that raises the chicken, as well as wholesalers and retailers, and consumers, who could buy cheaper poultry. Is such an outcome ethically acceptable? Who shall decide?

Rather than just messing with the genes of a particular animal, there is also the possibility of blending the genes of different species, perhaps adding in some human genes as well. These are referred to as "transgenetic" organisms. Many bits of human DNA are now inserted into mice for the use of science.[3] What will the future bring? Global science is not under the control of the US Congress.

GloFish were created more than a decade ago by scientists in Singapore who injected genes from sea coral into zebra fish eggs. The resulting fish had bright, fluorescent colors, and passed them on to offspring.[4] It is, of course, ironic that this extraordinary power, the accumulation of centuries of human scientific advancement, was exercised for such a trivial goal. It is a classic example of the results of mixing the economic forces of capitalism with new knowledge. What is the outcome for the fish? Is the birth rate and survival rate of the young better or worse? Is the quality of life changed? Do the fish live longer? Does the change cause pain or suffering? What happens when, not if, the fish is released into the waters of California or Asia? (Glowing is not a good trait when it comes to avoiding predators, but the fish may have other protective characteristics, for example, a bad taste.)

The questions around genetic engineering are significant and unsettling. The issues call for caution and wisdom, but it is more likely that the desire for commercial products will drive the activity. The point for this book is that this capacity is fundamental to demonstrating that humans are the information species, for good or ill. The guidelines suggested below are some initial thoughts about how respect might apply in the context of creation.

ETHICAL CONTEXT FOR GENETIC CREATION OF NEW ANIMALS

These are suggestions about the context in which to judge respectful creation and use. Genetic modifications:

1. Shall not result in beings that can live in only artificial, human-controlled conditions, such as cages or windowless buildings.
2. Shall not increase or eliminate the capacity for an animal to feel pain.
3. Shall respect the natural form and beauty of the species' parent stock.
4. Shall not decrease the intelligence of an animal.
5. Shall not mix the genes from different species unless it is highly probable that the outcome will be stable beings with a good quality of life.
6. Shall not be solely for novelty and entertainment. (It seems that those who care least about the welfare of animals are the most willing to create new life to profit by the novelty of it.)
7. Shall not occur without an evaluation of what would happen when the new being escapes human control into the natural environment.
8. Shall, in the case of commercial animals, be in the direction of less dependency on humans, not more. Self-sufficiency for the new being is preferred over dependency.

Beyond the issue of new animals, there are the issues of genetic manipulation of humans. This is more complex, since it touches closer to home. It gives rise to religious issues, and even the need to define what it means to be a human. By manipulating genes, can we make the human species healthier, smarter, or longer-lived? Can we add wings or gills? Should we? Why not? Can we, will we, reinvent ourselves, as gods who can engage in self-transformation?

We have no social consensus on these issues, no law providing positive directions. It is clearly an issue of the future. First steps were taken in the United Kingdom in 2015 when a measure was adopted allowing a child to be composed of the genes of three adults.[5] It is unclear what event will finally produce the full social discussion of all that is involved.

To say that we are the gods of today on this earth, with enhanced powers of creation and destruction, does not suggest how this will work out over the next one or two hundred years. Should the human species be viewed as if it were a four-year-old child with a loaded, hair-triggered gun in its hand, or like a forty-year-old man who has respect for the power of the gun? How much death will the human species inflict upon itself and the others of the planet before our power is harnessed, before wisdom and respect become the guiding paradigm for the individual and for the communities we inhabit?

> **We are the gods.**

CHAPTER 14

DEALING WITH DEATH

The Wave of Life: And You Think You Are So Important

An individual life is everything,
to the individual.
An individual life is not much
to the Wave of Life.

Pushing through time
the Wave is not self-aware.
In the good centuries
the Wave members propagate,
the Wave grows.
In the bad times it contracts,
but pushes on.
Second by second,
life by life,
millennium by millennium.

A single precious Wave,
with billions and billions of members.

Some species try to ride the top,
But forever cannot be done,
regardless of strength or numbers.
The Wave churns and turns.

The Wave is good, and I am glad
To be part of it,
To be aware of it,
To contribute to the next
turn of the Wave.

Come ride the Wave,
Help the Wave move through time.
Where is the Wave going?
Upon what shoal or shore will it break?

I shall not see that time.
It had a beginning,
Must it have an end?

> **If you promote more life,**
> **you also get more death.**

A FEW DIFFICULT DEATHS

On August 7 at about 3:00 p.m., the neighbor John had had it. The dog, Big Red, who lived next door, had been barking in the backyard for over an hour. And this was the third time this week. John got his pistol out, went into his backyard, and with a shot to the head, instantly killed the dog. Or maybe the story went that he put poison in a hot dog, threw it over the fence, and four hours later Big Red was dead.

How should we think about the ethics of what was done? Was it or should it be illegal? The actions of the dog barking were a negative state of affairs for John; did it justify the action taken? Most of us, having had some level of experience with dogs, generally would say no: such actions are disrespectful, an unethical balancing of the interests (as well as a violation of criminal cruelty laws). Big Red had his fundamental interest in continued life; John had his interest in getting rid of the annoying barking. John did not acknowledge the dog as an ethical subject, feeling that his interest in being relieved of an annoyance was paramount. John did not feel the need to balance anything; he just took action. We turn to our holistic judgment, the quick judgment of right side of the human brain, and say that John was wrong in his action, that a balance should have occurred, and that other, nonlethal options, were available. The law will intervene in this case after the fact. Under property-law concepts, John is financially liable for the destruction of the dog because it was the personal property of the owner. However, in most states the amount recovered is only the market value of the dog at the time of the destruction, plus some veterinarian fees. Under the criminal anti-cruelty laws of a state that make it illegal to kill an animal unnecessarily, he is at substantial risk of being guilty of a felony. But the level of punishment actually imposed in such a case is very hard to predict.

Death by gunshot to the head is very different from poisoning. It can be assumed that the poison, over the four hours or so before death, caused the dog great suffering. If John had acted in this manner, the ethical condemnation should be even louder. Death is one issue, suffering another. Poison will predictably produce suffering, and the intentional infliction of suffering would very likely be condemned as unethical conduct by an even wider group of people. Our culture accepts animal death all the time; it almost never accepts the intentional infliction of unnecessary suffering. Beginning in 1887, states have made it illegal to poison animals.[1]

On August 20, John's sixteen-year-old son, Nero, was found in a vacant lot, watching a cat burn to death. Nero had poured gasoline on Tabby the cat, and struck the match. The cat lived for a day but died because of the high degree of burn injury. When asked why he had committed the act, he said he was curious what the cat would say and do, and it was just a feral cat anyway, so who would care?

This act demonstrates such a high level of disrespect that near-universal condemnation would be expected. Saying that it was unethical is not nearly descriptive enough. Such actions are outrageous. The degree of suffering was very high; so high, in fact, that we become convinced that there is something truly wrong with Nero. We expect a "normal" sixteen-year-old to know enough of the world to recognize that such an act is completely unacceptable conduct. We conclude that there is something psychologically missing or off in the brain of Nero and the act stands as a warning of significant risk of future bad acts against animals and even humans. The nature of Nero's interests, his curiosity, does not justify the suffering and death of the cat. Of course from the animal-welfare perspective it makes no difference if the cat has a human owner or not; the duty of respect is owed to the cat itself as a living being and a moral subject, not the owner. This is not a justifiable death.

On September 15 at 2:00 in the afternoon, John's dog, Ned, is picked up by animal control for biting a four-year-old child the day before. Ned caused significant injury to the face and right arm of Shelia. It occurred in the middle of a public street, and there did not seem to be any provocation by Shelia. Three days later, a hearing is held before a magistrate to determine if it was Ned that caused the harm, which in fact had been caught on a cell-phone camera. It was also determined that this was the second such attack and that Ned somehow had gotten out of John's backyard fence. The court ordered the dog destroyed; two days later, the dog was killed by lethal injection.

It can be assumed that the death of the dog was lawful, since it was ordered by the court. But was it ethical? This is a different type of problem, and it raises the initial question of whether the actions of a state actor can be judged in an ethical context. This will be considered in some detail in a later chapter, but for now assume the answer is yes. The state also has the power to condemn human beings to death for inappropriate acts, so there is no question that the state has the power to kill an individual, be it a human or an animal. It is the social ethics of the people within the state that will decide whether to exercise that power.

Is the death of the dog to deter acts of violence by other dogs, to punish the dog, or to protect the public from further risk of violence? The killing of one dog will not deter other dogs from biting humans or other animals. While some may consider punishment to be a compelling justification for the death of the dog, the primary motivation is probably protection of the public. The dog has shown what it will do, and the owner of the dog failed to do what was necessary to keep the dog confined. The harm that a dog can cause to human bodies is not trivial. It is possible that removing the dog from John's ownership and placing it elsewhere might allow the dog a third chance to harm someone. Can the dog's inappropriate behavior be corrected? Not all are. So the death of this dog might well be found to be an ethical decision. The interest of members of the public in not being injured or killed by the dog Ned outweighs the interest of Ned to continue living. Even so, it would not be ethical to torture the dog before killing it for the harm that it caused. Death and suffering are not the same. Intentional infliction of suffering would not promote any public good and is itself a public negative. (Note that society does not demand the destruction of cars that kill humans. Why?)

What about the person who gives Ned the lethal injection? It is by definition a lawful act, but is it an ethical one? These are separate questions. Perhaps to the person euthanizing Ned, it is just a job; he might "put down" ten dogs a week for any number of reasons. What if the person goes out of his way to make the last day for the dog as positive as possible by giving Ned food and attention before administering the lethal injection? In judging the human in this case, do we look at his motivations and emotions, or just at the effect of the act of killing the dog by injection?

I admit that the preceding discussion shows threads of speciesism. I did not consider the dogs and the humans equivalent. I did not suggest a death sentence for John or his son for the death that they caused. Again, not making them equal is a holistic judgment, arising out of my life experiences; perhaps your judgment would be different. How would you go about explaining to yourself, if not to others, why it would or would not be different for the dog that harmed the human to die and not the humans who killed the dog? Opening that door may well raise many other questions. Recognize that all of the above arose in the context of the community of companion animals, giving extra weight to the life and well-being of the animal in question. Now let's change the community context.

END-OF-LIFE DECISIONS

Death is also an issue in the community of companion animals: they grow old or experience heath issues such as cancer. All who have had companion animals for a long time come to that point in the animal's life when death is near, the animal's quality of life diminishes greatly, and the likelihood of future suffering increases. Should we wait and let the animal die naturally, or should we allow death to be induced by a veterinarian? Many owners do not wait to let nature take its course and at some point seek to eliminate the animal's suffering by allowing an induced death. Is this ethical? So long as the decision is a judgment about the animal's best interests, it is not unethical. But of course complexities can arise. The owner may simply be tired of dealing with an older animal; he is no longer the companion that he once was. The cost of healthcare may become burdensome. The more that the decision is based upon the interests of the human, the closer to the unethical line the decision becomes.

On a number of occasions, elderly humans have provided in their wills that their pets should be "put down" upon the owner's death. This is usually based upon the belief that no one else will care for the companion animals as they do and that only suffering would be in the animal's future. While the owner of property normally has the full right to dispose of the property at his or her death, the law has decided that this is one wish of the owner that can be set aside.[2] The implied wish of the animal to remain alive supersedes the wish of the human owner and, where possible, alternative homes are sought out by the executors of the estates.

ZOO QUESTION

Let us turn to the local zoo and the Brady family. While passing by the tiger exhibit, the oldest son asks: "What do they feed the tiger? Maybe they could put an antelope in the cage every few days so the tiger can kill and eat the antelope right here where everyone could see it; that would be awesome!" Well, it is true that the tiger needs meat and would naturally kill an antelope or equivalent as its source of protein. So there is the broader question, is it ethical for a zoo to hold animals for display that require the death of other animals to feed the display animals? What if there were surplus antelope at the zoo and something must be done with the extras? (Presume the exhibit was built for ten antelopes, but because of births over the past two years, there are now fifteen in the exhibit.) What if it was beef from a local slaughterhouse? The son's suggestion of letting the tiger kill and eat prey animals in its enclosure at the zoo is a different or second ethical question. Letting zoo visitors see the death would offer a more realistic understanding of the nature of the tiger and what happens in the wild. But we humans don't like to actually see the death of our meat or someone else's, so most likely the zoo would say no just because of the "sensitivity" of predator humans who are in denial about the natural world.

We hope that the managers of the zoo consider the interests of the prey animal in question (the antelope or the cattle that provide the beef) and their duty of respectful use in making decisions about what to feed the tiger. They are the gods who determine which animals live and which die at the zoo; how each animal shall live and obtain food; and when and in what manner each animal shall die. If they decide that the surplus antelope should be dinner for the tiger, then they can also decide how to humanely kill the antelope, under their duty to minimize pain and suffering.

If you want to see life at the zoo, there will likely be death as well.

Does that change your mind about the ethics of having such entertainment? Does the fact that none of the animals are companion animals shift the weight of the interests of the animals? Does it matter whether the animals in question are cute, cuddly creatures (like penguins or koala bears) or less attractive ones (say, a hyena, a vulture, or a python snake)?

How are we to judge the breeding of feeder mice sold at the local pet store to be eaten by pet snakes that must kill their prey or consume it alive? Why do we let individuals keep "pet" snakes at all? (Increasingly state laws limit the ability of individuals to keep dangerous animals, and this often also includes the big constrictor snakes.[3])

LOCAL WILDLIFE QUESTION

Now let's focus our attention once again on the local park that has an overpopulation of deer (see chapter 10). Is it ethical to kill deer in order to realize a better ecological balance of that local ecosystem? Assuming that there is no other effective method of reducing or keeping the deer population at a sustainable level, then it is ethical. The interests of the individual deer have to be balanced against the interests of all the other animals inhabiting the same park. We must accept that since we humans have created an artificial condition for local wildlife by removing some natural predators, we have a duty to protect and preserve the habitat for all wildlife. Controlling the deer population is not just ethical, it's a duty for the humans in charge.

THE ACT VERSUS THE MOTIVATION
FOR THE ACT

There was a criminal case that arose out of the death of three iguanas in New York City in 1996, which offers a pointed example of how human motivation can be considered separate from the death of the animal. The defendant was charged with violating the state anti-cruelty law by cutting off the heads of three live, conscious iguanas without lawful justification. These killings were performed in his apartment and were intentionally videotaped. After the animals were killed, the defendant prepared the bodies as food and ate as least some of the meat. Shortly after the event in the apartment, the tape of the beheadings was submitted to a local television show under the heading "Sick and Wrong." The tape was broadcast on the show. The man was found to be in violation of the law; apparently the trial court jury held that the primary motivation for his action was the publicity he would garner, and in fact did receive, by getting his tape shown on the television show. The jury did not consider this motivation of sufficient social merit as to justify the deaths. It was a group holistic judgment.[4]

The defendant's attorney pointed out that iguanas were killed on a regular basis in the city at various restaurants to provide human food, and that no one in the restaurants was charged with a crime. Additionally, he did indeed eat some of the meat. Also it might have been noted that there was very little suffering, as regardless of how bloody the scene might have appeared on tape, the quick loss of blood to the brain brought almost instant unconsciousness and then death to the animals.

The criminal case was appealed, and the higher court wrote an opinion upholding the criminal conviction while focusing upon the critical phrase in the statute, "unjustifiably kills." The court held that it was not justifiable since the deaths were not to preserve the safety of property or to overcome danger or injury.[5] Clearly, the death of the animals for human publicity purposes is not a socially acceptable reason and is therefore unjustified. The court did not directly address the death of animals as a source of food. But, if left to a jury, it is doubtful that the death of an animal would be considered unjustified if the purpose was to provide food for humans. Of course, any vegan or vegetarian could also point out that eating iguana meat by anyone is not really necessary and likely not supported by the science of nutrition. But the culture of eating meat is stronger than the science of nutrition.

Asking if any particular negative action is unjustified is to ask a social ethical question. The members of the jury would bring their sense of the ethics of the community into the jury room as they decide whether the acts are a crime. What do you think; was his act unethical? Should he go to jail? In the end, this is an example when it is not the death of the animals that determines the outcome of the judgment, but the human motivation for the deaths that is weighed. What do you think about that?

DEATH BY PLANT PRODUCTION

Ethical vegans seek to harm no animals as a result of what they purchase. This is done by careful consideration of the contents of anything that may be eaten or purchased. Their goal, focus, and efforts are ostensibly to be admired, but they do not always see the full story. Avoidance of commercial meat can be considered appropriate in the context of the industrial food system that most agricultural animals are part of in the United States. This system has been shown to create considerable human and animal suffering as well as environmental harm. The present industrial food-animal community is an inherently negative community. But this is not the place to set out all the animal suffering of the existing food-animal system.[6] For some humans, the conditions in which such animals are raised is not the issue; they simply do not want to be the cause of an animal's death. And, I accept that as a positive ethical position.

However, in the broader context of this book, the focus of the vegan is too narrow, while other visions of the animal agricultural system might have positive ethical points. While vegans seek to avoid the animal industry of today, if they eat soy, wheat, or corn, they are fully immersed in the global industrial agricultural system with all of its herbicides, pesticides, and fertilizers that also cause death and suffering.

In planting a field of corn or soybeans, there are a number of unseen costs, direct and indirect, to other lives. The most egregious costs arise the first time a field is put into mono-crop production. Everything, from fence to fence, above the ground is killed and removed or plowed under. This act is a total negation of our duty to support the community of local wildlife. The entire local food chain is destroyed: the insects, frogs, snakes, moles, rabbits, and birds. The predators that use this food base must move on or die, and many will have nowhere to go.

The ongoing cost of creating fields of corn or soy is the opportunity lost to create a diverse group of crops or, even better, a pasture that supports honey bees year round, and supports sheep, wild rabbits, moles, and a host of other animals. Complexity is better for life; it provides a richer place to exist. We pay a significant ecological price for the economic efficacy of mono-crop production.

Besides the initial direct cost to life, there is the reality that the petroleum-based fertilizer used in industrial agriculture has pollution and resource-use consequences where the chemicals come from, where they are used, and where the pollution ends up. There now exist annual dead zones off our coast where the agricultural chemicals, carried by the spring rains to the oceans, kill off the marine life near the mouths of rivers. Our mono-culture farming that uses industrial chemicals is the source of all of this marine death.[7] To eat grain is not to avoid being a cause of animal death. How many local environments are harmed by the runoff of topsoil and applied chemicals from the surrounding farmlands? How many animals die as a result of this pollution?

In time, the soil in these mono-crop fields is destroyed. Soil is an unseen ecosystem that is critical to the support of all the plants and the animals above the ground. It is a rich, diverse, and complex system. Existing mono-culture farming extracts the resources, the soil nutrients, that are there, but it does nothing to improve and protect the ecosystem of the soil in the long term.

Vegans may have been able to reduce the number of food animals within the industrial-animal food system, but they are financial supporters of a system that kills and eliminates local wildlife and their ecosystems, as well as causing local and long-distance environmental problems. Of course, since it is almost impossible to know from where the grains we consume were raised, it is difficult to identify the place where this harm is happening, but it is happening regardless. Those who seek out organic grains support a slightly better outcome, as the crops themselves are not treated with poisons, but they are still mono-crop fields. The clearing of those fields also eliminated the diversity of nature's living creatures.

If we have a duty to all of life to support its flourishing, then the existence of mono-crop production should be avoided. There is a common counterargument that if we are to feed the exploding human population of the world, the "efficiency" of mono-crop production is required. That is a topic that is worthy of a separate book, so I will not fully address it here; however, we can consider one alternative. What if there were a system that eliminated the negative pollution and the petrochemical consumption, protected and supported local wildlife, provided protein for human consumption and an income for families, and aided a good life for domestic agricultural animals and a positive lifestyle for humans? We have to go back in time to find such a system.

THE DEATH OF FARM ANIMALS IN A PASTURE-BASED SYSTEM

For millennia unknown to us, our ancestors ate meat as part of their diet. For most of this time, it was a simple act of survival. But today the eating of meat has to be evaluated within an ethical context, because the animals are now to be considered ethical subjects and humans have other food options available to them. This brings us to the most difficult of questions arising from our analysis: can any human use that results in the death of animals for purposes of human consumption be considered respectful? The short answer is, in my holistic judgment, yes; but it is justified only in limited circumstances. The death of an animal is a negative for the animal even if it has lived a respectful life. Therefore, there is a consider-able burden to show the positive effects that such a death will provide to others. Other factors must be present so that the human desire to consume animal products and our pleasure in doing so is not the sole benefit to be realized from the death of the agricultural animal. Human pleasure alone is not a sufficient justification for causing the death of another being.

For those of us in the United States, the animals in question are the usual ones found on Old MacDonald's farm: cows, pigs, horses, chickens, sheep, goats, and so on. Note that in the nursery rhyme there is no mention of death. And farms that use the term "Old MacDonald's farm" are usually zoos or sanctuaries, not working farms with the killing and slaughtering of livestock as a reality of the cycle.

The following factors all contribute to the creation of an ethically acceptable community, where the raising and keeping of food animals in a pasture-based system is justified because of all of the positive outcomes for the animals, the environment, and the humans:

1. A premise not yet realized: The death of any animal within the system is humane.
2. A premise to be more fully realized: Farms are occupied by the owners of the animals, who also deal with the animals every day.
3. The management system utilized in such a community ensures the health and well-being of the animals present, meeting both their mental and physical needs. The life of the animals is not in a state of suffering.
4. The animal is able to experience most of its natural interests and DNA-driven capacities. This cannot happen if an animal is con-fined to a cage or a building for its entire life.
5. The management of the fields of the farm will support some habitat for the lives of local wildlife.
6. The food coming out of the system will be healthy and nutritious for humans.

7. The ecosystems on and off the farm will not be polluted. Soil ecosystems will be enhanced and protected.
8. It is a positive environment for the humans engaged in the enterprise.
9. It is capable of making a living wage for the humans engaged in the enterprise. The raising of animals is serious work, not a hobby; for it to accomplish all of the above at a level to have a positive and notable impact on our agricultural production, it must be profitable.

There exist already physical contexts in which the above factors contributing to an ethical community can be realized: pasture-based farming. This is a place where a positive community of commercial animals exist.[8] This may or may not be organic farming. "Organic" has issues not relevant to this discussion. Instead, the concern here is that it be pasture-based. The grass is green. The grass is good. Grasses (and trees, etc.) are the critical boundary between the unseen in the soil and the life, our life, above the soil. The pasture ecosystem is robust, complex, and environmentally sound.[9] It does not require pesticides or herbicides; and with the recycling of nutrients from animal waste, it requires minimum fertilization. The ground is always covered, and rain and snow will not erode the soil.

Those human characteristics that defined the development of the United States: self-reliance, independence of thought, ability to solve problems, and so on, were honed in the process of the western migration and settlement of this country. Multiple-species, pasture-based farming was the historical model. We need to return to that, but with all of the information and insight that science can now provide.

A pasture-based, multiple-species farm is a very complex enterprise. Not everyone can do it. It requires organization, financial resources, commitment, focus, flexibility, science and technology, and good neighbors. It is seldom an enterprise that can be taken up by one person. It is hard physically and mentally, but if the challenge can be met, it is very rewarding. On a nice sunny day standing in your pasture (which may have taken several years to reach full health) and watching your animals grazing contently can provide a level of satisfaction that is hard to describe. It is a holistic sense of satisfaction, of creating positive outcomes. It builds supportable self-confidence and pride. But even as you stand there, you know the peaceable kingdom will not last for long. Either the animals or the weather will challenge you with a new problem.

Consider the existing industrial system in which corn is planted and harvested with very large, expensive equipment, and shipped hundreds of miles for processing. The processed corn is shipped to confined facilities around the country and fed to cows that don't have a digestive system that can accommodate corn.[10] Why not plant grass, alfalfa, and clover, and let the animals eat where it grows? Of course, the adoption of pasture feeding on the full scale would destroy or modify significantly our existing industrial agricultural system. But I see that as a positive.

We need to resettle the country if we are to achieve this goal. Hundreds of thousands of city dwellers need to return to the land to seek the goals and values set out in the previous chapter.

The case for the humans is fairly easy to make. But what about the animals? Pasture-based farms will help the local wildlife community, but the linchpin in this enterprise is the agricultural animals that are brought into existence to be used by humans. Is it ethical to bring into existence animals that will have a good daily life but a premature death? Is it better that the animals be born and used in a human food system than not be born at all? We are the gods. It is our decision, our responsibility. Assuming that their life is good and their ultimate end is not foreseeable by the animals as they live day to day, then their shortened life is justified with all the other positive factors that arise in pasture-based agriculture. This is not the same matrix in which ethical decisions about companion animals are to be made. Animals are primarily defined by the community in which they live, and in this case they are animals being raised as food.

RESPECTING ANIMALS

Reflections on My Farm

There is a goodness, a quiet acceptance of their life in the daily rhythm of my sheep. With no fear or understanding of the future, they take each day as it comes. Rising with the sun while the grass is still wet, they walk quietly, single file, out to pasture to find their daily food. Eating and being with others, they sit in the shade if the day is hot, chewing their cud and drinking water when necessary. They do not bicker with each other or worry about world affairs, but head butts do occur to establish and keep the order in the flock. Strength of will is present even if they are only grass eaters. Domination is an occasional issue, but it gets worked out. Repetition is not a negative for them; I don't think the word boredom *applies to them. A few days a year, there is the excitement of sexual arousal, the routine is broken, and lambs are eventually on their way. The rams walk away without a care; the ewes have the heavy duty of raising the young, with some doing better at it than others. On our farm they have not had the fear of predators to deal with, but the occasional shot of a gun during hunting season does disturb them momentarily. In the snow they sit, satisfied with life, especially since we bring the hay to them. Some will seek us out for a scratch, perhaps, but most come to us hoping for a hand out of beet pulp, the chocolate of the sheep world. Another summer arrives, the pattern is the same, and they seem satisfied with their life. Surely all of these good days outweigh that one bad day. It is a day of sadness, as no premature death is easy for those responsible, but it is a day necessary to make the ecosystem work. To use the product of death requires the creation of life, and the wave rolls on.*[11]

A CONVERSATION WITH KAREN

At a hearing in Washington, DC, in 2006, I had the opportunity to meet Karen in person. In the animal-rights movement, she was the go-to person for chicken and other agricultural bird issues. During a brief and pleasant conversation, I told her that I had recently obtained some Icelandic chickens and was enjoying learning about them. Her first question was, "You're not slaughtering them, are you?" I said no, because we had not yet done so, and I did not think it possible to explain in a few sentences why we might. Instead, I talked about how fascinating it was to watch the chicks with their mothers and hear all the interesting sounds they made.

At her farm, a rescue center for chickens, Karen said they could not let the eggs hatch, so there were not any chicks. I don't know if this means that they don't have roosters, they keep the sexes separate, or they simply collect all the eggs. I suspect this rule of no chicks is because her facility would quickly run out of space. Her comments clearly juxtaposed two views of the world, that of animal rights and that of sustainable agriculture.

Karen's farm has individually named chickens. She has put agricultural animals into a near companion-animal community setting. While this provides an apparently idyllic life for the chickens present, it deprives the hens of their critical life task of raising chicks. This approach creates a disruption of the genetic flow of their lives. The hens will die without passing on their genes, which amounts to a genetic failure. At our farm, by contrast, mostly unnamed chickens, including brooding hens and baby chicks, engage in the full life experience, including fights over territory and hierarchy. But we end up with too many roosters; after they reach sexual maturity, their constant sexual activity will exhaust the hens and cause feather loss and trauma. A ratio of one rooster to five hens seems best for the health and happiness of our breed. One solution is to humanely kill and eat the roosters. If you want to promote life, you must accept the fact of death as well. We humans are the gods who decide which animals live, which hatch, and which ones die. We replicate nature in being the predator, the killer of the genetically unnecessary roosters.

Figure 14.1.

Occasional Very Short Stories Series

Transformation

Harold is sitting on the patio with his friend Glen, with a tall beer in hand. It is the quiet time of the evening when the shadows and soft, warm breeze encourage contemplation and deeper thoughts. From the patio they can see out over the east portion of the twenty-acre front field, which is dark-green with two-foot-tall soybean plants.

> **Harold**: This field, when pasture, used to support four steers, twenty sheep, five hogs, and two hundred chickens. They grazed the grasses and the weeds, manured the field, and sat under the trees on the edges. The field also supported thousands of insects, one

hundred thousand or so worms, six rabbits on average, one fat groundhog, hundreds of mice, a dozen snakes, fifty toads, one hundred frogs, and fifteen songbird families. Frequently, the local hawk and fox would come by for a lunch. I hated to mow the field for all the disruption it could cause. So sometimes I would leave sections alone. Would you believe that our straw-bale hut for the chickens not only had the expected family of mice in residence, but one year a pair of garter snakes actually raised a family under the straw wall?

Glen: Sounds like you had a lot of death, one animal eating another, that sort of stuff.

Harold: If you want life, you have to accept death. If you promote life, more death will follow. I don't know any way around it. It doesn't seem like avoiding causing death is a good enough reason to not promote life. But of course the Transformation arrived about three years ago, and farm animals are no longer allowed. So I joined the crowd and plowed the field and planted soybeans in hopes of selling into the expanding tofu market.

Harold pours more beer and finds chips for both.

Harold: Glen, it has been three seasons now, and while I am able to make a little profit on my land with row crops, I find myself often despondent, unsure what to do, and unhappy with where life has taken me.

It seems so strange to me that those who assume a motivation of compassion toward animals have created an outcome that reduces life's destiny and diversity, builds nothing for the future, and takes the joy out of my life.

At first, row-cropping was an exciting challenge, new skills to learn, new machines to buy and operate, and a new rhythm of the year to adopt. I admit to pride in the furrowed field with dirt all smooth; pride when the planted rows of green peeked up out of the soil. During the hot August days the plants are a beautiful sea of dark green, and the wind can ripple the plants like the surface of water, entrancing the mind. With fall comes the anticipation of harvest and the anxiety of whether the yield and sale price will produce sufficient income. After all our hard work, would it come together? That first year, the elevator operator was amazed at my yield, but when I told him it had been grazing land the year before, he nodded and then shook his head, saying, "Well, don't expect to see this yield again." When I asked why, he said the land still had the richness and diversity of a healthy soil ecosystem, but that in short order it will lose that richness and my crops will become entirely dependent upon annual inputs of fertilizer and herbicides and pesticides, and that worms and microorganisms will die off from lack of organic matter and food.

Two crows circling in the sky catch his attention. His eyes lose focus, then he gathers it back.

Harold: Am I better off? Are my lands and the neighboring river better off? Are the animals that no longer exist better off? Is this progress? Have I supported the Wave? I think not.

This past winter, we had a heavy rain and I watched my topsoil being washed away because there was no grass to capture and hold the water, to protect the soil from the power of flowing water. After the rain, I took a walk and found little two-inch-deep gullies. Where did my soil go?

Then, this spring, just before planting, I was in the field and gathered up a handful of soil and was depressed again. It wasn't the same. You know, when soil is good it feels sensual in your hand. Healthy soil isn't dirty. It holds together. It has a cushion; you can compress it and when you let go, it springs back. You can feel the life in it. This time it just compressed into a mud ball with no life in it. It's a shortcoming of significant consequences today that so many millions of Americans have never held good soil in their hands, to feel and see the source of our food chain, the lining of the lungs of the earth.

So, Glenn, I have been thinking while sitting in that tractor seat, which policies should we pursue: maximizing corn and soy output or maximizing life diversity, soil richness, and stability? How much does the quality of *my* life count in all this? I say, let's return to a system that provides milk, meat, and wool from sunlight, water, and grasses; supports soil and ecosystem diversity; and allows so many others to cohabit my modest plot of land. It's enough to make me a Civitist-Democrat.

The sun is sinking on the horizon and the first fireflies appear in the dark shadows . . . and the beer glasses are empty.

DEATH OF ANIMALS IN SCIENCE AND TESTING PRODUCTS

The number of rats and mice that die every year in the name of science is not discoverable by a member of the general public, which includes me; hundreds of thousands certainly—a million? Who knows? How do we think about this issue: Is it ethical to develop genetic strains of animals that are more disease-prone (e.g., cancer susceptible) than normal strains? Is it ethical to inflict a condition on animals that results in pain, suffering, and death? Is it ethical to test new commercial products on whole live animals, resulting in suffering and death? It is much easier to state the issue than the answer. Our existing society is based upon the information science has gleaned from the world around us; science pursues information and insight. While considerable amounts of money are part of the process, it is the information gathering that is the justifying human value for the conditions and death imposed upon the animals.

While I am comfortable with understanding scientific information and the general process of science (with my undergrad degree in chemistry, I only opened the door), I am not part of that world. I am a law professor. While I am comfortable with my position on agricultural animals,

RESPECTING ANIMALS

I am not in a position to suggest a comprehensive answer to the ethical dilemma posed by science and animal research. Here are a few of the questions and problems that need to be addressed before a holistic judgment can be rendered:

> Distinguish the quality of life before and after an experiment, the quality of life during the experiment, and the nature of the death.
>
> Understand that the nature of experiments is that the results and the usefulness of the experiment cannot be known in advance; it is, after all, an experiment. Some animal experiments produce no useful information. Some animal experiments produce insights and information not even expected at the beginning of the experiment.
>
> To the extent that an experiment seeks information that might be applied to human issues, is the information really transferable? Are biological processes of a mouse really like that of humans? Is it a closer case for rats? (What does that say?) Chimpanzees are the most like us, but today there are no terminal experiments with them, and indeed they are being phased out of formal science, without any changes in law but with changes in the ethical view of those within science.[12]
>
> Considerable funding from both government and private sources is part of the university science-grant process. Individual human egos as well as institutional prestige are also part of the mix.
>
> Congress has wisely decided to make no judgment about which scientific pursuits should be undertaken, but it has set rules for the housing and living conditions of animals before and after the actual experiment.[13] Is this the extent of our ethical obligation?

I am open to believing that some terminal use of animals in science could be ethical, but I am not in a position to suggest where to draw the line. However, using live animals in terminal testing for new commercial products is not science and not justified in today's world. The European Union has outlawed the use of animals for cosmetic products. It is hoped that very soon new, alternative testing technologies will allow the entire practice to disappear.[14]

A SAD SHEEP STORY

As must be clear by now, I know and like sheep. About a decade ago, a speaker came to an animal-science department presentation at Michigan State University. There had been some experiments in the United Kingdom with a flock of sheep to ascertain their mental abilities. It was observational science, with no infliction of pain or suffering. It was very interesting, and of course the sheep were shown to have a certain mental robustness not previously expected. Afterward, I approached the researcher and asked what had happened to the flock of sheep. He said they were all killed after the experiment. I was very sad.

Death after the experiment is perhaps the most unexamined aspect of the use of animals by science. While chimpanzees now have retirement options, there is no retirement home for rats and mice after their use. It is almost always death.

DEATH BY HUNTER

Another difficult area is the ethics of killing wildlife in the context of sport hunting. I have never hunted and did not come from a hunting family, but I have known many good people who are hunters. Decades ago, I gave up having arguments with hunters about their killings; it was not useful, and instead it produced much more emotional heat than light. But, over time, I have come to a rather-simplistic position on the issue. If the motivation of the hunters is to boost their egos and their self-esteem, to experience the adrenaline rush from causing the death of another being, then the practice results in unethical and unjustified death. Wildlife should not die for the entertainment and self-satisfaction of the hunter. Trophy hunting is a subcategory of sport hunting in which the motives appear to be personal pride in causing the death of another being and then the need to display that death to demonstrate the worth of the hunter to others.

What I have come to understand is that the motivations for killing wildlife in a sport context are extremely complex and personal to each individual who confronts the topic. To attack sport hunting generally can be perceived as an attack on family values, on experiencing the wilderness, on seeking ecological balance, on obtaining food for the family, and on the values and history of how the United States was settled. There is also the problem that arguments against hunting run into the quagmire of gun control. I have also come to understand that the positive hunting ethic seeks to impose no suffering on the animal, just a quick and clean death. Of course, it does not always happen that way, and some methods of hunting make a clean kill less likely than others.

While, as with science, there is considerable money that is part of the activity of hunting, money does not drive the motivation to engage in the practice. But those who make the money do seek to promote the culture of hunting. This extends to the state agencies that regulate hunting and sell hunting permits, since much of their financial existence depends on the activity of hunting. The cultural and community context is more important and much more complex in the minds of the hunters themselves. Because my dividing line requires me to look into the mind of each individual as a trigger is about to be pulled, I cannot know who is the ethical hunter and who is not. This is truly personal to the individual. All I can ask is that hunters have a reflective conversation with themselves about why they hunt.

As a result of we humans having removed the primary predators from most ecosystems in the United States, hunting plays a significant role in population control. What is the balance of interest among all the wildlife against the death of some herbivores? Might it be more ethical to cleanly kill a deer that has had a natural life than to buy pig meat when the pig has suffered for most of its life in the agricultural animal-industrial complex? As with agricultural animals in a pasture-based system, the determination of ethical conduct must be made in a broader context than just the death of a particular animal. Human motivation is important, as is the ecological context.

All of this can make a person's head spin. The issue is not subject to rational, logical analysis; there are too many variables, and each individual will make his or her holistic judgment.

THE AIRPLANE-FOOD DILEMMA

A dilemma: I do not want to promote the existence of caged chickens or pigs and therefore do not buy the meat of animals kept in such conditions. I fly regularly and have my meal preference marked as vegetarian so as to not consume the meat of industrial animals that might be served. However, the serving of preordered meals has disappeared as the major airlines compete in a global marketplace that values only cheap tickets. My problem is that, as a frequent flyer, I occasionally get upgraded to first class, where they do serve a meal on the longer flights at the right time of the day. The airline no longer adjusts the food provided based on those filed preferences (except on international flights). Sometimes one can choose a vegetarian selection if a choice is offered. But on this particular day, there was only one option and it was placed pleasantly before me with a smile. Among other things there were slices of ham on the plate. My choice was clear: eat the ham or don't eat the ham. If I don't eat the offering, the meat goes in the trash as waste. My choice was not going to provide any feedback to the pork producers. I, of course, was clueless as to where the pork came from and the conditions under which it was raised. Admittedly, I did not need the calories and I previously liked the taste of pork. The question before me was, Do I honor the pig's life and death by eating the meat and acknowledge its contribution to my day, or would I honor the pig by refusing to eat the ham and allowing it to go into the trash?

My Contribution

The Wave knows me not,
But I know the Wave.
What might my contribution
Be?

Some Humans weaken, diminish,
Reduce, risking
Life, diversity.

So I must
Keep the genes flowing,
Share the awe,
Promote, create, protect
Life today, tomorrow.

And with my mind
Spawn and focus
Ideas, perspectives,
Most passionately,
With strength to
Motivate action, inaction.

Enhance the Wave.

> Sometimes the decision of death is acceptable, but then there is the method of death.

CHAPTER 15

DO ETHICS OPERATE WITHIN OR UPON GLOBAL CORPORATIONS AND GOVERNMENTS?

H aving developed an understanding of how humans engage in ethical judgments and acts, and how animals can and should be part of our individual ethical world, a significant difficulty remains. There are two major institutions or communities that can have a significant impact on the lives and welfare of animals, yet they stand apart from the world of ethics. Do corporations and governments operate with a self-derived ethical compass? Even though they are composed of humans, they do not always act as an individual human might when faced with ethical choices.

In the world of law, corporation and governmental entities have a visible presence. They may file lawsuits and be sued; they are legal persons. Are they persons or ethical actors in the world of ethics? They are not living beings; instead, they are the accumulation of the subparts of large numbers of humans. They are not alive and therefore have no interests apart from the humans who compose them. Are they ethical actors? Well, they certainly have the capacity to understand that their actions or inactions impact humans outside the corporation, as well as the environment and animals. They also have the capacity to direct their actions to be more or less respectful of ethical subjects such as humans or animals. (Whether corporations can be ethical subjects is equally complex.) To the extent that corporate leadership is strongly held in one individual human, then the corporation may well reflect the ethical judgments of that specific person. The focus of this chapter is not on the closely held corporation created by an individual or family. In these cases, the shareholders and the decision makers are exactly or nearly the same and the leadership can decide to make less profit in order to be appropriately respectful of others—including animals. Also, this discussion does not deal with ethics within the corporation and issues like the treatment of women or minorities. Rather, the concern is specifically about corporations' relationship to animals and the general environment in which they work.

The focus here is on the megacorporations in which there is significant separation between the shareholders and the management of the corporation. In such cases the ethical perspective of a single individual does not guide the decision-making nearly so much. There is significant shift in context. Emotion, empathy, and the capacity for holistic judgment recedes, and accounting becomes the language of the community. The human desire for profit becomes dominant. The individual human transfers this desire to the corporation but does not transfer all of the other components of being human. Instead of building positive communities, megacorporations seek profit under the rules of capitalism. There are business judgments to be made, not ethical judgments. However, a business judgment may be about ethical issues (e.g., "should we clear-cut this forest in order to plant corn?").

Likewise, it is not respectful use that drives governmental entities; the rules of politics do. The context for judgment within the world of politics is that of seeking or keeping power or control over humans, animals, and resources. The drive for power, like the drive for profits, can become so dominate in some individuals that negative ethical consequences have little weight in the decision-making. Respectful use is not realized. Clearly some who seek and obtain power do so in an ethical context that allows and promotes respectful use. But in others it clearly does not.[1] Unelected government employees are limited and rewarded within the confines of the laws adopted by the elected officials and the desire to retain their jobs. Both elected officials and government employees do not exist in a world that promotes respectful use of others.

While both corporations and governments may act in respectful ways toward individual humans and animals, it is not a primary goal of their existence. It would be a huge mistake to expect either corporations or governments to engage in self-reflection and determination of future actions based upon the ethic of respectful use. When, as in China, some business corporations are controlled by the government, the problem is magnified. Respectful conduct toward humans, animals, or the environment by these organizations usually requires the constraints of law. It is possible that respectful use will occur because of customer demands on the corporation or voter demands on the politicians. Note that both entities may well have very ethical individual humans who are part of corporations and governments. But the culture of both entities often frustrates the application of ethics to the actions actually undertaken by either form of human organization. They are not individual ethical actors, but they may have much more power to impact the lives of animals and the environment than you or I.

THE NATURE OF LARGE CORPORATIONS

A corporation is an artificial legal entity created as a method of combining individual human assets (such as money, land, and ideas) while limiting the individuals' liability or responsibility for the acts of the legal entity. A corporation allows for, but does not require, a separation between those who provide the assets by investing in the enterprise and receiving stock in return and those who manage the enterprise (e.g., the chief executive officer [CEO], the chief financial officer [CFO], chairperson of the board, etc.). There are other forms of business enterprise such as partnerships, but they are not really relevant on the global scale, even though they are driven by the same rules of capitalism.

The goal of the corporation is to return to investors more money than they initially invested. We will not address managers who cheat the corporation, diverting its assets for their personal benefit with multimillion-dollar salaries, but for the purposes of our discussion we shall assume that management in good faith is seeking to provide a profit to the investors.

When one corporation operates in a niche of the economy, it normally has a few competitors striving in the same market. For example, if the corporation provides timber to homebuilders, then there are likely to be a few corporations competing for the dollars of the many homebuilders. One corporation may provide better lumber, another lesser-quality lumber but at a lower price. Another will specialize in hardwoods. Perhaps customers will support all of these approaches, perhaps not. This is called competition. It is the nature of the competition between business entities that is a fundamental part of the enterprise of capitalism.

Capitalism in the past century competed with a bastardized version of communism and state socialism as alternative methods of resource allocation. The victory of capitalism (combined with democratic governments) showed that nonpolitical, noncentralized business decisions produced the best economic outcomes, that is, better-quality products in greater abundance and at a cheaper price.

A corporation cannot decide how big an army should be, whether the drinking age should be twenty-one, or the level of taxes to be imposed upon individuals or corporations. Those are political decisions to be made by a government, which is a political community, not a business community. The goal of the political enterprise is to respond to the needs of those citizens who live within a particular political state. As it is the state's law that allows for the creation of corporations, the state has the responsibility, and indeed the duty, to control corporations. The corporation has no right to control the state.

(I know I have not yet said anything about animals or the environment. Just hold on, this is not easy stuff, so I fear a more-detailed introduction is necessary.)

GLOBAL CORPORATIONS AND GOVERNMENTS?

There is an inherent conflict between the goals of a government and those of a business enterprise. Critical to success in the capitalist world is keeping the cost of production at a minimum. But many of the techniques used to reduce costs run counter to the goals of the government to protect other, noneconomic interests of the citizens, for example, the well-being of children. Almost one hundred years ago, the United States made a political decision that its young citizens would be best served if they obtained an education rather than if they worked in factories or shops for cheap wages. Thus, an ethical position about the use of children was imposed upon corporations by the operation of law. This helped realize the social goal of an educated population but increased the cost of production for corporations that had previously used child labor. Corporations exist not to provide social good but to provide products (e.g., cars, potato chips, and CDs) at the highest possible profit margin.

Within the United States, all corporations had to abide by this rule prohibiting child labor; as a result, some experienced an increase in cost, and the consumers paid more for some products. The corporations had to find other strategies to control or reduce costs. The same dynamic has played out for many issues related to the welfare of the people who work for corporations (e.g., the minimum wage, maximum work week, etc.). So long as the economic market and the reach of the laws had more or less the same boundaries, then the human social rules did not cause large advantages or disadvantages to those within the marketplace. Additionally, the benefit and the burden of the laws were realized by the same set of people, the citizens of the United States. But the new world of globalization has caused a new complexity for corporations. It is illegal to use child labor in the United States, but it is not illegal in many other countries, thus creating for the cost-conscious corporation an incentive to move its manufacturing activity to the less-regulated and lowest-cost country.

The awaking of the United States environmental movement in the 1960s occurred when people realized that many, many corporations were producing unwanted by-products, wastes that were simply dumped into the air, water, and ground. This kept the cost of the product low but, as the science of the time began to show, it did so at a destructive cost to the environment, even affecting the people who had to drink the contaminated water and breathe the polluted air. Citizens decided that this destruction of the environment was wrong and therefore directed their legislatures to impose laws upon the operation of corporations to protect both themselves and the environment. At the time, a number of corporations wailed that these restrictions would lead to their demise. And so it was for a few, but most corporations adjusted to the regulations. New laws were catalysts for some corporations to find alternative methods of production that reduced pollution and kept costs low. (Paper production is an amazing, if now old, story of new engineering solutions to difficult pollution problems—capitalism at its best—once society told producers what level of pollution was acceptable.[2]) Again the ethical beliefs of citizens caused the government to restrict the options of the private corporations. But this is okay since corporations exist within a social-political context that ought to limit their operations if they are viewed as detrimental to the society.

CORPORATE MOTIVATION

How could the negative conditions under which industrial egg-laying chickens live have come about?[3] What is it about the nature of corporations that lets them not only accept unethical living conditions for the hens, but also promote this industrial mode as a moneymaking model for the world? The answer to these questions is critical as we seek to shape our future and give focus to the political action and legal changes that are necessary to move forward. This same inquiry will also show us why megacorporations have the potential to inflict harsh consequences upon humans and the environment.

The first step in understanding capitalist corporations is to understand the rules under which they exist and grow.

RULES OF CAPITALISM

1. *Maximization of profit is the golden measuring rod. Not only must there be profit, the profit must be an increasing level of profit—if not quarterly, at least annually.*

   Mixing this point with the reality of globalization produces examples such as IBM, which in December of 2004 announced that it was going to sell its computer-manufacturing division to a Chinese firm. Consider the motivation for the sale. IBM had decided that although the division was profitable, higher profit was not available since sales would be driven primarily by price competition and volume and thus increasing sales and high profit margins were unlikely. So it was not that computer sales were not profitable, but that the sales were not sufficiently profitable enough. For IBM, sales of services represented the best potential for growth of profits. The Chinese firm that purchased the division, Lenovo, immediately became the third largest PC maker in the world. Capitalism marches on.[4]

2. *Wherever possible, replace human labor with capital investment.*

   Machines don't require sick days or retirement plans. Depreciation of capital investments can often be accelerated, thus increasing short-term profit; labor costs can seldom be accelerated for tax advantage; and future labor costs like retirement and medical benefits remain uncertain but will undoubtedly be large, thus reducing future profit.

3. *Simplify. Seek uniformity in products and methods of production at the level of quality that the market will support.*

4. *Seek economies of scale. Bigger is better because it allows for the largest capital investments and the realization of cost efficiencies in management, advertising, and other parts of business practice.*

5. *Eliminate competitors. Consolidate and get bigger; most products and services need only three to six global producers.*

There are only two makers of large commercial airplanes; six companies control 80 percent of the world market in automobiles; and so on, with computer printers and airlines for instance. Most recently the process has been working in the area of agriculture and seed production.[5]

6. *Shift market risk to suppliers.*

There was a time when the US auto companies made many, if not most, of the parts that went into their automobiles. But over several decades the companies divested themselves of these functions. This was, in part, to avoid the labor costs, including health and retirement benefits, of the people making the parts. It was easier to seek outside suppliers than to reduce their own cost structure in which unions had the power to support the workers. It was the only real way to allow price competition, to bring down the cost of the parts themselves. But once spun out, the stand-alone parts firms were caught in a squeeze. In 2005, Delphi, GM's major parts supplier, filed for bankruptcy protection.[6]

Thus, much of the risk of capitalism is borne not by the auto company but by the smaller enterprises, their workers, and share-holders. If these US corporations cannot perform, then parts companies in China will undoubtedly step forward. Indeed, one of the strategies of the US auto-parts companies has been to take the production process to China before Chinese companies can figure out how to get into the US car-parts market. This is fully appropriate conduct under the rules of capitalism, even if it results in job losses to US citizens.

7. *Play by the rules: the rules of the stock exchange, the rules of accounting standards, and, if it can't be avoided, the rule of law.*

This is taking the high road; the low road would argue that

corporations will play by the rules only if the positive consequences outweigh the negative consequences, that is, on accumulation of profit. For example, human corruption is an economic inefficiency to be avoided if possible, but corruption is sometimes less costly (more profitable) than is playing by the rules.

8. *Give out as little information as possible.*

Increasingly, public corporations are required to disclose information about the nature or impact of their products (e.g., smoking causes cancer), and there has been a countercurrent of corporations going private.

Note that increasing the quality of human life, preserving the environment, and respecting animals do not make the list. Do you see why not? But, remember, I said that capitalism is the best economic system available.

> The larger and more global the corporation, the less likely that it will be constrained or directed by noneconomic values.

CORPORATE LEADERSHIP

A key element in understanding the human world around us is to understand how and why corporations make decisions that negatively impact human labor, the environment, and animals. It is important to separate out the personal beliefs and ethics of the individual humans outside the corporate setting and the context in which they have to make decisions within the corporate setting. As an example in history, consider the railroad barons of the nineteenth and early twentieth centuries: Andrew Carnegie, Jay Gould, and Cornelius Vanderbilt. This was a period of unrestrained capitalism. While many of these men ultimately did a number of public good acts after they had cumulated their wealth, any description of the business process used to obtain their initial wealth would contain words such as *ruthless, unconscionable, union busting,* and *environmentally destructive.* For almost a century, laws in the United States have constrained much of the early negative effects of corporations, but the issue has arisen again in this century, with much more complexity in our new global capitalist context. Corporations are created in many other countries. It cannot be presumed that those individual humans as part of the governance of foreign corporations share the ethical view of those of us in the United States, and, indeed, they may well operate under a very different set of laws about animals and the environment, or under no laws at all on these issues.

When profit becomes the dominant value in an organization, what happens to the individuals contained therein? A decision maker in a corporation can be like a member of a slow-moving and well-dressed mob. A mob enjoys freedom from personal ethical responsibility, a freedom from normal personal constraints or beliefs. Its members face pressure to behave in accord with the culture of the mob, the corporation. The actions of a mob may make sense within the mob but be diametrically opposed to the actions that individuals within it would take on their own. The corporate director would never personally pour petrochemical waste in a river or look into the eyes of a thirteen-year-old and tell him his wages for the day will be fifty cents or confine a hog to a lightless pen, as they do in confinement agriculture. Instead, others within the corporation act on the behalf of the corporation: time, space, and displacement of acts onto others are the buffers between the decision maker and the repugnant actions. The corporate culture is a soothing salve for individuals who might otherwise shrink from their own actions.

A successful decision maker in a corporation is one who accepts judgments on the terms of the corporation. Profit is the god, good ethical outcomes are not. Ethically correct outcomes are not inherent in the corporate structure; they are not the ultimate measure of corporate success;

they are not the reason for corporate existence; and they are not measured or reported to the board of directors. Concern for ethical outcomes is the realm of religions, philosophy, and governments only when citizens have effective control over the composition of government. Corporations exist in the world of money, supply and demand, and economic efficiency. They are constrained in action and outcome by those laws that the corporation must obey. It is the duty of the state to protect and seek ethically good outcomes while capitalism is at work. That is why the government needs to pass laws to constrain the corporate dragon. (Many small, local corporations do operate with the ethics of their owners when the corporation is really an extension of an individual, particularly if the founder is the executive of the corporation. My concern is global corporations. Additionally, there has been a movement for the past few years to have corporations assume some social responsibility. We will see what happens.)

It is important to acknowledge one feedback mechanism within the capitalist system that can impose respectful use by corporations. If their customers demand it, then it might happen, but it has to be customers with significant leverage over the sales of the corporations. For example, for decades individuals and nonprofit animal-welfare organizations have been trying to change the conditions under which egg-laying chickens are raised. Their one big success has been in California, which now requires somewhat-better cages for the birds.[7] But, in 2014–2015, some of the big purchasers of eggs, like McDonald's and Walmart, announced that their suppliers would need to change the living conditions for the egg-laying chickens.[8] The egg producers will listen to this because failure to do so might significantly reduce egg sales. The welfare of egg-laying chickens should improve. This is an unusual example of one corporation forcing better animal welfare on another corporation in the absence of law. While a number of animal organizations have pushed this approach for a long time, I believe the suppliers' actions occurred only after the issue of hen welfare had gained in importance not only to corporate customers but also to the individuals on the egg suppliers' boards. I also suspect, but do not know, that they received information that in taking this act, their cost structure would be impacted at a low level.

Understand that the risk to the corporation in ignoring profit and seeking ethically positive outcomes is that other corporations will not, and thus the latter group will be more efficient in producing lower-cost products. Therefore, the ethical corporation will lose (either close up, be bought out, or go bankrupt) in the only playing field that matters: the marketplace. For instance, how many of us are willing to pay one thousand more dollars for a car so that the company can pay lifetime health benefits for its workers?

Corporations are the economic engines of today's society. It is wrong of us to judge them otherwise. They are essential in the critical task of efficient allocation of resources so as to create wealth, for individuals, for societies, or for the entire globe. But to ignore their character is to allow a bull loose in a china shop. Something fragile will be broken. It might be a person's health, an animal's chance to live without suffering, or the purity of a stream. We do not want to kill the bull; we want to constrain it so that it can perform its job without harm to others. The pen for the bull is constructed out of legal planks.

This critical view of corporations is not meant to suggest that they do not sometimes do ethically good things. But, with only a few exceptions, such good acts are done only when the corporation perceives its own benefit in the act. Judgments of right and wrong do sometimes affect corporate action, particularly when a public image will otherwise be harmed and sales drop (e.g., Nike and the use of third-world child labor[9]). Those who run a corporation know they can polish its public image with ethically good actions. But if directors do not make a profit for shareholders, they will not long be around to run anything.

We may need more inefficiency in our capitalist system. The capitalist system rewards efficiency of production, which normally creates profits and accumulation of wealth. But protection of the environment, protection of workers from exploitation, and animal welfare are also goals for our community. They reflect values that actually run counter to those of capitalism. Fairness is not a value of capitalism per se. The well-being of the planet or a species or individual animals is not a goal of capitalism. Assurances of basic health needs like clean water are not goals of capitalism. Human rights and reproductive freedom, even freedom of the press or freedom of religion, are not values of capitalism. Yet we humans hold these values most highly. The protection of these values is a reason for the existence of government, to ensure our mutual well-being, at least for those who accept democratic principles. To adopt provisions that constrain corporations may make the capitalist system more economically inefficient. If protecting workers, animals, and the environment result in higher costs, then so be it. The difficulty arises in seeking an acceptable balance in a political system awash in corporate money.

But the government must also recognize its limitations. It does not make good economic decisions; it is an ineffective and inefficient wealth producer. One lesson from the last century is that economic well-being is not best left to governments. The positive wealth effect that we want includes the creation of a middle class with its political stability, the protection of human rights, and sufficient tax income to help provide human needs and protect the environment. But as corporations generate wealth, it gives them considerable power and political influence. They can't vote, but corporations can use their money to influence outcomes in the political process. Corporations create a political counterweight to citizens who seek to limit corporate operations because of a desired social good or outcome. Corporations grasp the process of lobbying.

In the United States, historically, we have done as good a job as any, perhaps even the best job, in balancing the benefits of capitalism with the noneconomic needs of citizens. Each state or region of the world establishes a different balance between the strength of the state in asserting the interests of the citizens in maintaining a clean environment, in less work, and in more pay against the strength of corporations' efforts at getting more work from employees, with less pay, and fewer benefits. Old Europe, with its more socialist outlook, has perhaps constrained capitalism too much, and its corporations may find it harder to compete internationally. The Chinese win a number of economic battles because they give almost no protections to individual workers (a curious outcome for a Communist government) or the environment. There must be a balance within each community. It's hard to believe that China will not move to protect workers, and the environment in which they all live, over the next decade. But I fear that animal-welfare issues are not given the same level of concern. Time will tell.

What do you think would be the public reaction if a candidate for the presidency of the United States made a speech as follows:

Political Speech by Then Presidential Candidate Carol Remmy, July 4, 2020, in Washington, DC.

This evening I have decided to address something a little more abstract than any particular law. I think it might be useful to reexamine the role of the government in fostering the ethical development of its citizens—this government that I am seeking to lead.

A government is based upon the needs and desires of the people for which it is formed, to be the shepherd of a diverse and dynamic flock. Thus, we protect ourselves from external threats with a military and have created a law enforcement and legal system for social stability and fair dealings within our society.

But what of the spiritual needs of the people? What is the role of the state? This country was founded with the realization that there must be a separation between the government and the organizations promoting specific religious beliefs. It is not the role of the government to impose a religious perspective on each individual; the choice of religious beliefs is a personal decision for each citizen. Our Constitution, and specifically its first ten amendments, seeks to protect the individual from those within government who would impose their specific perspectives on others. But does this mean that the government has no ethical perspective? Can it not act to promote an ethical outcome? I think there is a necessity for a strong ethical perspective in our government actions. The balance is to draw from the ethical beliefs of the diversity of our citizens without preaching a particular religion. For example, in the United States we have strong ethical beliefs in the equality and self-worth of every person. This is also a fundamental thread of many religions and philosophies. If a person comes from another part of the world where the prevailing belief is that the husband or father has full control over wives and children, then their behavior must be modified in our country. In the United States, the abuse of a child or wife is not acceptable, ethically or legally. It is through the legal process that citizens reach consensus as to the ethical perspective of government and law. It is a fundamental strength of the United States that our law represents a consensus arising out of a great diversity of personal beliefs.

One value maintained by most religious organizations, and for that matter by many without religious beliefs, is the importance of the family as the premier social unit. As such, it is appropriate and necessary for the government to support the family unit. It is in the context of the family that the fundamental information and values for a satisfactory life are transferred from one generation to the next. Our history is rich in the role of families: immigrant families, pioneer families, slave families, wealthy families, and political families. Ideas such as honesty, fair dealing, respect for others, self-sufficiency, self-reliance, confidence, the value of work, and the necessity of sacrifice for the family are at the core of beliefs widely held in our society and therefore should be reflected in our government policy. Yet it seems harder and harder for the family to function in its traditional role, with all of the competing claims upon time, distractions of peer pressure, and corporate intervention, by means of marketing, into younger and younger lives.

The government must balance the desires of the corporations for profit and efficiency with the needs of families for protected space in which the time-honored process of fostering values can take place. While many aspects of this issue might be examined, tonight I want to look specifically at the loss of the family farm as a place for values to be nurtured and transferred. What has happened to the family farm? It has largely disappeared over the past forty years. We have an agricultural industry but not family farms.

I believe that getting meat and potatoes a little cheaper is not sufficient reason to eliminate this historically important context for the
development and transmission of traditional family values. Certainly
the farm life can be a hard life, and it is not for everyone, but we—both
individual citizens and the government—ought to preserve the option
for those who wish to live as did so many in generations past. We must
eliminate the barriers to family-level entrepreneurship in farming. We
must return to local markets as a significant source of meat and produce.

The organic foods movement must be supported, so that labor
and care are rewarded with higher value in the market. There should be
limits on the size and vertical integration of the food industry.

Fair and open labeling is necessary so that we understand where
food comes from. It is time to outlaw cruel conditions of animal confinement in the food industry, to say that no chicken can be kept in a
cage for its life. Doing so would take away the economic advantages held
by the megacorporations and eliminate their abuse of animals. Limits
on animal densities need to be established, for the betterment of these
living creatures, those that raise them, and the environment. We need to
see a broader space for the multiple-species family farm where children
work with their parents, to give a time and a place for the transfer of those
values and ideas that this country was founded upon.

As your president, I will seek this and other ways to return family
farming to the forefront and, within this social context, our traditional
values can be conserved, and our freedoms continue to flourish.

As a starting point for discussion I propose the following:

CODE OF RESPONSIBILITY FOR
ANIMAL-OWNING CORPORATIONS

1. The natural life of the animal shall be the benchmark by which
   conditions are judged.
2. Individual life shall be respected.

3. Quality of life and swiftness of death shall be discussed and understood at the executive and board level.

4. All executives and members of the board shall visit unannounced (monthly for executives and quarterly for board members) an animal-production facility controlled by, or under a source contract with, the corporation.

5. Any board member of an animal-owning corporation shall be required to possess compassion for animals. (I know, I know . . . but it's my book.)

A final thought on government decisions. The political process within a democracy ought to allow for the concern that the general population has for the welfare of animals within their various communities to be transformed into government policy by the adoption of laws. And this has occurred. The states of the United States have a large number of criminal laws in place to protect the welfare of animals. But if we focus on the activities that are exempted from the law and the goal of good animal welfare, we are apt to be discouraged. The presence of overwhelming amounts of money in the political process and the desire of those holding elected political power to keep power by the drawing of boundaries of election districts is significantly reducing the feedback loop that elections are supposed to provide the citizens. I have no specific answer for this concern, but I suggest that the concept of respectful use of animals cannot be fully implemented without invigorating the right to vote and the consequences it should have on those holding political power.

Control the Dragon

CHAPTER 16

A FORAY INTO THE LAW

It is now time for a brief and hopefully painless foray into the realm of law. The bridge between personal ethical decisions and law is a bit tricky, even a little risky. In most democracies, if enough people believe an action, like dogfighting, is unethical, then they can make a social statement by the adoption of a law that outlaws the activity. This is society deciding on what is acceptable personal conduct and in so doing taking away from the individual his or her prior right to act upon personal beliefs. Thus, ethical positions can become law, but are all laws ethical? Since there is no external objective standard by which to judge the moral nature of an act, the judgment must be viewed as a personal one. In my mind, the answer to the above question is no. Some laws are ethical, some are not, and others have no particular impact on ethical subjects and therefore are not subject to ethical analysis.

I may strongly believe an activity is unethical. But you may disagree. We may have an argument and seek to change each other's mind. Or if you have political power, you may choose to simply ignore me and pass a law that will make my belief irrelevant to the broader society and force me to change my conduct (but of course a law cannot force me to change my belief). For example, the issue of human abortions is an ethical issue with strongly divergent views within our society, and both sides seek to trump the other's ethical view by the passage, repeal, or litigation of laws.

Laws exist as the result of the exercise of political power, however that might be defined within a particular country. Clearly, the keeping and obtaining of political power often does not reflect any attempt to balance the interests of animals against the interests of humans. The small-cage confinement of egg-laying chickens was lawful everywhere in the United States until about ten years ago and represents a near-total suppression of the interests of the hen over the profit making of the corporations. Who had the political power? What would the law be if the chickens could write the law?

But this chapter is not about political power, it is about the presence or absence of animals in the legal system and how they could have an enhanced presence in the legal system. This chapter is also not a short course on animal law[1]; rather, it is an opportunity to expose you to some new ideas that can facilitate change in the legal world such that the law will better respect animals. I seek to enhance their presence and visibility in the legal system because at the moment I believe their interests are not adequately represented. That is, too often the legal system either ignores or does not give sufficient weight to the interests of animals.

LEGAL PERSONALITY

Historically, with animals as property, the law viewed animals as objects about which humans had legal rights and responsibilities. Animals were not the holders of any legal rights or responsibilities themselves. Therefore, the threshold question in the arena of law is whether or not animals should have any presence in the legal system as holders of legal rights. The simplistic answer, the one most often espoused within the animal-rights movement and elsewhere, is that animals have no legal rights. It is true that at the moment animals are not allowed to file lawsuits in their own name.[2] This is because in order to file lawsuits, the individual or entity must have the characteristic of being a legal person, that is, the ability to be a recognized actor in the legal world. (Just like in the world of ethics there are ethical actors.) And, of course, it is the legal system itself that decides who is a legal actor. A stark example of this from our darker past is the US Supreme Court case concerning Mr. Dred Scott. In this case,

Mr. Scott sought to use the legal system to challenge his property status as a slave. The Supreme Court, however, held that because he was a human slave, he had no legal status; the law did not see him as a legal person with the capacity to file a suit on his own behalf, and the case was dismissed.[3] With the elimination of slavery came the elimination of that category of "nonlegal human persons." In the United States today all children and adults are legal persons by simply being human. The difficult conceptual question before the courts today is whether or when a human fetus is a legal person in possession of some or all human legal rights.

This special status is also given to "others," such as cities and corporations. All of these others who may file lawsuits are really just groups of humans whose particular interests have been gathered together under the umbrella of entities such as cities and corporations. Because these groups have legal personhood status, the law is very careful about defining what group of people may use that umbrella. There are very specific rules in the law about how to form a corporation, and if you do not meet the rules, then you cannot declare yourself a corporation. There are also legal oddities such as ships and the estates of dead people, like Elvis Presley, which have legal personality. But really these are just clusters of human economic interests. In the end, it must be said that the legal system appears to be entirely human-centric, in that the ability to access the legal system to intentionally assert legal rights or to protect oneself from others is reserved to individual humans or groups of humans.

So, if animals are not legal persons within the realm of law, what are they? They are property, personal property to be more precise. (The other property categories are real property [land and buildings] and intellectual property.) Let us return to the living room of Homer and view the scene through a legal lens. Homer is a legal person; an actor with visibility in the legal system. The ball is property; a human is the owner of the ball. The owner of personal property, as a general rule, may do as he wishes with his ball: he can sell it, give it away, play with it, eat it, destroy it, bury it, or enshrine it in a gold case. In all such cases, the law does not care and will not intervene. The ball is an "it" in the eyes of the law, not a legal person. Remember, the presumption is that the human has the right to do as he wishes with property unless specifically restrained by law. In no sense can it be said that Homer has any legal duty toward ball, just as he has no ethical duty toward the ball. So the law is mute on the issue of whether to kick or hug the ball.

Homer's son is a human and therefore a legal person. His son has legal personality, legal visibility in the legal system. The son has legal rights that impose obligations on others. Note that this is the case even though the son has not sought the status and is entirely unaware of the status. It is a gift to him by our legal system for simply being a human child. He does not have the full set of rights that will be available when he is an adult, and his obligations to others are also very limited, but he does have legal personality. Therefore, the law has a number of things to say about how Homer should or should not interact with his son. The son's rights impose limitations on Homer's actions. The son has the right to be free from physical injury and trauma. Homer has the duty to not impose physical injury or trauma and to provide adequate care.

Since Homer does not know what he will do after he opens the door, the law is not helpful at this point except as a possible restraint on bad acts as Homer holistically weighs what to do. If he hugs his son, then the law remains silent; there is no duty to hug and no punishment for not hugging. If he kicks his son, then the law will have much to say after the act has happened. The law, through the prosecutor's office, may file criminal charges for assault and battery. Another part of the legal system may begin an action to revoke his status as a parent and remove the child from the home. He is in trouble. The son is not an "it" but a legal person. Therefore, it is also possible that a civil lawsuit might be filed against Homer in the child's name, to recover money damages for the harm, the pain and suffering, inflicted upon the child by Homer.

Now what about the dog, Rover? It might be said that since Rover is personal property, then the law will treat *it* like the ball and not like the son. But that is incorrect. Beginning in 1867, in the state of New York, animals have had a hybrid status a little like the ball and a little like the son. Under this law, which has propagated since then into every state in the union, a human may not cause an animal unnecessary pain and suffering.[4] Under the scenario previously set out for Homer, the law would have a slightly different perspective than an ethical analysis. It is a reasonable assumption that a jury would find that the kicking of Rover is the unnecessary infliction of pain or suffering and therefore that a crime has been committed. Depending on broader circumstances, such a criminal act could result in jail time or a criminal fine and might include mandatory counseling for anger management. What cannot happen in the world of law is that Rover may not file a civil suit against Homer to obtain money damages for the pain and suffering. So is Rover an "it" or a "he"?

Itness

Demeaning, sexless
Would you like to be
An it?

Lowest, respectless
Is your cat
An it?

Grammar, reflecting
Legal status.

Animals have sex,
Deserve respect.

Companions are
He or she.
So are chickens.

LIVING PROPERTY: ANIMALHOOD

When the status of something is uncertain, the old-time saying is that they are "neither fish nor fowl." In this case, the fish and fowl are neither entirely personal property nor human legal persons, rather, a bit of both. This causes jurisprudential confusion. How are we to think about animals? Why has this confusion arisen? It is because as a society we acknowledge that animals do have interests (as in the interest not to be harmed by humans), and we have placed that acknowledgment in the anticruelty laws. There is no anticruelty law for balls or cars or computers, because they do not have any personal interests; they are not alive. But, on the other hand, animals are not humans. The weight of centuries of having animals strictly as personal property lays heavy upon our legal thinking. Indeed, going back in time, many animals did not even have the dignity of being considered personal property, since only animals with economic value (e.g., work animals, show animals, and the like) were protected by the law. Messing around with the fundamental categories of property is not lightly done; many judges will not allow it in their courts.

There is one simple way to clear up this confusion. Animals need to be removed from the category of personal property. Some might suggest that animals simply be merged with humans and become juristic persons. While this is possible, and it might well be what happens in a few hundred years, an intermediate step is required at this point in time. For over a decade I have been urging in my legal articles for the creation of a new category: living property.[5] This category would be a formal acknowledgment by the legal system that animals are different from other objects (e.g., balls and cars) and as living beings they deserve a new, distinct status in the legal system.

Nonliving Personal Property **Living Property**

tables, cars, & books **dogs, cats & chimpanzees**

Figure 16.1.

There is one country that has already done this. In the Swiss Civil Code (Article 641a), it states: "Animals are not chattels" (an old term referring to tangible, movable property, e.g., personal property). However, the Swiss law having removed animals from the personal-property status did not create a new positive status for them. It is a bit awkward to say that my dog is "not chattel." What, then, is he? I would respond by saying, "He is living property with animalhood within the law."

The point of having a new category is to create a new blank slate where we can thoughtfully create new rules of relationship and legal rights for animals without confusing things or insulting humans by claiming there is no difference between a dog and a human. Within this new space change will come slowly, issue by issue, or species by species, or community by community. It is expected that some legal advantages for companion animals may be adopted that are not available to animals in research. This is the case because it is the nature of law and legal change that it comes in pieces, paragraph by paragraph as the legal system grinds through the political law-making process. While many in the animal-rights movement wish for an abrupt change that will be for all animals simultaneously, that will not happen. There will not be a civil war fought over this issue, no sweeping elimination of property status for all domestic animals. The best we can expect is that the political process will deal sequentially with the various human-animal communities.

WILLS AND TRUST

The formal use of wills and trusts to set aside financial assets for the support of companion animals exists today as a widely accepted concept that can easily be moved into the living-property arena. It is representative of the future integration of animals into the legal system. The law of wills has been developing for centuries in the common law countries. The English statute first allowing wills to transfer title of property was adopted in 1540 during the reign of Henry VIII. Until very recently it was not possible to leave any money in a will at your death for the benefit of your companion animal, or any other animal. The quick historical justification was that you could not give property (money) to property (the dog) and that such a grant would violate the Rule Against Perpetuities (don't ask). But, over twenty years ago, the creative thinkers in this area of law decided that there was not really a public-policy reason to prohibit a widowed pet owner from leaving some money for the care of her life companion, be it a cat, a dog, or a human. Recognizing that a companion animal could not handle its own money (just like a human child could not), the mechanism now available in most states is the expressed creation of a trust within a will that designates a human trustee who has the duty to take care of the money and distribute the money for the benefit of the identified animal.[6]

Although it is not known how many companion animals have had trusts created for them by their humans, the notorious hotel owner Leona Helmsley created one that received front-page news coverage after her death. The New York billionaire created a trust, effective at her death, with $12 million in it for her beloved Maltese dog. A judge later reduced the amount to a mere $2 million, which apparently was sufficient to support the dog until his death several years later.[7]

The existence of these laws represents the reality that the legal system has the capacity to acknowledge and protect the interests of individual animals. While it does not allow the animal in question, denoted as a beneficiary in legal terms, to file an enforcement lawsuit in the animal's name, humans may file suits on behalf of the beneficiary animal to ensure that the will is adhered to. This is a key example of animals having some status in the legal system, but not full personhood. It is important to have a name for this status. Animals are not full juristic persons who have personhood within the law; but they should be considered to possess animalhood, defined as a set of live beings who have a presence in the legal system, which requires for at least some issues an acknowledgment of their interests, which will need to be weighed against human interests by the legal decision maker.

HUMAN DIVORCE

Another area of the law, which is now being drawn into our new living-property arena, is that of companion animals that become intertwined in the divorce proceedings of their humans.[8] If you talk with judges who deal with divorce matters, there are many stories about how important custody, visitation, and support issues for companion animals can be to some humans going through the process of divorce. It is evidence of the growing importance of companion animals to humans as the family unit shrinks, with fewer or no children, and the animals become increasingly important to the emotional central core of the human family.[9]

The legal difficulty with existing divorce law is that in almost all states animals are considered just property, and resolution of disputes about the animals will focus upon ownership of the property. The laws of these states do not specifically allow the courts to consider what is in the best interests of the companion animal caught in the middle. If the husband bought the dog, then the husband has the first claim to the dog, regardless of the future capacity of the husband to care for the dog, or who was previously the caregiver within the home, or with whom the animal had the strongest attachment. (I am ignoring community property states, which can be more complex.) In contested divorces, animals become pawns in the conflict.

There are two exceptions to the above discussion. In 2016, the state of Alaska amended its divorce law to give legal visibility to companion animals.[10] The Alaska law allows the relevant court to make specific determinations in a final divorce order about companion animals:

> (5) if an animal is owned, for the ownership or joint ownership of the animal, taking into consideration *the well-being of the animal.*[11] (Italics added.)

In 2017, the state of Illinois also amended its law with the same result.[12]

These laws are a clear acknowledgment that an animal in the midst of a divorce has interests independent of the spouses—that the animal has legal personality to be seen and considered by the legal system when a divorce proceeding impacts its life. This acknowledges that an animal within a family is in the conceptual position of a child (both have interests but cannot self-advocate for those interests), and the court has an independent duty to consider the best outcome for the animal, rather than the wishes or property ownership by one of the spouses seeking the divorce. Other state legislatures have now also seen bills submitted that would change the laws in their state.

EQUITABLE SELF-OWNERSHIP

(Note: This section is more for the lawyer than the nonlawyer.) Our legal system already contains some concepts concerning owning or holding title to something, which can be used to support the idea of a new legal space for living property. The British common law, which is foundational to the US legal system, has long allowed the title of property to be divided into two parts: legal and equitable. Let's return to the case of Homer.

When Homer sets up a trust for his son and places $10,000 in the trust for his education, then the title to the money transfers to the trust (which has independent legal existence) and the son is considered to have equitable title (a legally enforceable interest in the money, but not full control).

One or two steps away from this legal construct is the idea of companion animals having equitable self-ownership. Their animalhood within the law can be seen as an equitable self-interest supporting a legal personality, while acknowledging that a specific human also possesses legal title. The human has a legal interest in an animal at the same time that the animal has an equitable interest in him- or herself. This legal construct also supports the idea that the human would have direct obligations toward the animal, as the legal title holder in a trust now has obligations toward the equitable title holder or beneficiary.[13]

If we can say that humans are self-owned (where legal and equitable title come together), and I think we can, then it is possible to say that the animals are partly self-owned, halfway between human status in the legal system and the nonstatus of personal property such as tables and cars. This would give them sufficient legal presence that the legal system would have to recognize the animals at some level. I am presently drafting a deed of dignity that would allow animal owners to create or acknowledge this new status for any animal they own. Stay tuned. Accepting this view of animals will mean that the law is more respectful of the animals, giving them legal status, legal visibility.

WHAT ABOUT WILD ANIMALS?

Wild animals or wildlife present a different kind of problem when considering their status in the law. Wildlife by definition are animals in their natural habitat that are not the property of any human or human substitute. This discussion does not cover wildlife in zoos, which are property. Also, in this discussion we will ignore the complexities of feral animals, particularly feral cat colonies. The focus will be upon Big Bob, a black bear in Michigan. Now, that is my name for him and I acknowledge that he has not had the opportunity to name himself (but then I did not name myself either). However, he is a specific bear. He was born in 2013 and has been fending for himself very nicely since he left his mother's care. He is smart enough to stay away from humans and is attractive to the female bears as a mate.

Figure 16.2. (Wikimedia Creative Commons, User: DaBler; licensed under CC BY-SA 3.0.)

Since he does not fit into any of the property categories, how does the law view Big Bob? Historically, wildlife have been considered things without title, *ferae naturae*, available for capture by any human, as is the water in the ocean. In common law countries, it is not proper to say the state owns all wildlife. Rather, the state asserts the right to control when and if humans may take possession of a wild animal. (The US government has even less control over wildlife, it being an issue usually reserved to the states.) If Big Bob were to decide to kill a sheep in the field of Joe Farmer, the state of Michigan is not liable for the value of the sheep under common-law principles for the harm done by the bear, since the state does not possess or control the bear. The state could decide to pass a statue allowing recovery of money for harm to sheep if it wanted to, but is not required to do so.

In the United States, each state has game laws that direct which species of wildlife require a permit to kill or capture individuals of that species and which species do not require a permit. In Michigan, a state-licensed hunter may kill Big Bob roughly between mid-September and the end of October.[14] The robust Michigan anticruelty law contains an exception for lawful sport hunting; as a result, the law of Michigan is mute about the degree of pain and suffering that might be inflicted upon Big Bob should he come within the sight of a permitted bow-and-arrow hunter. Also, the question of whether his death is necessary is set aside if the hunter has a permit and is hunting within the allotted time period. There is no place in the legal system where Big Bob may assert his interest to continued life or to the manner of his death.

One difficulty is that our present legal system does not think of bears as individuals, only as part of a group. Wildlife are given attention only as categories of species (i.e., endangered, game, threatened, or nongame) or as inhabitants of a place (e.g., the bears and deer of the Upper Peninsula in Michigan). He is only an unseen part of an indistinguishable group. While it is ecologically useful to consider these groups when making some decisions, it is time to also consider the pain and suffering of individual animals when it is inflicted by humans.[15]

So it is that wildlife will not neatly fit into the category of living property, since they are not property. But they are living, and while it is possible to change the name of the category to perhaps "animals," which could easily encompass both domestic animals and wildlife, the title "living property" seems more useful, and we should just wink and let the wildlife under the umbrella. It does make some sense because the primary concern of the legal system arises when humans seek to make wildlife their property, so to stretch the term would seem to be just.

In the case of wildlife, there is no need to go through the linguistic difficulty of declaring them as possessing the legal status of equitable self-ownership. Since no human is in possession of them and therefore cannot own them, they simply have self-ownership as might any human. Big Bob has the same capacity for independence, and self-direction, as does a human. He is responsible for his own food, housing, and reproduction of the species. He is an individual independent from humans, but an individual not recognized by the legal system at the moment. What do you think about that? How can we ignore the reality of his individual existence?

How important is it that this animal has a name? In the summer of 2015, a big-game hunter from the United States shot a lion with an arrow in Zimbabwe. He was a "beloved" lion with the name Cecil. Condemnation went viral and global. The lion had a name, a story, and pictures. He was easily identifiable by his black-fringed mane and a GPS tracking collar. For many people he was considered as a person. Very few humans around the world showed any concern over the deaths of the hundreds of other unnamed lions killed that year by hunters in Africa. Afterward, the hunter said that he would not have shot the lion if he had known it had a name.[16] Why is a name so important?

Remember, I do not seek a status for Big Bob of being a human in the legal system; I advocate just that he has visibility in the legal system—that he has animalhood.

WELFARE VERSUS RIGHTS

The animal-rights debate is fraught with misunderstanding, emotion, and definitional problems. When speaking in public I try to not use the term "animal rights," because in any audience there is a wide spectrum of response and understanding of what the term might mean. Remembering that we are in the world of law and not ethics, let us start with two points that we might all agree upon. First, no animal presently has the capacity to be named as a plaintiff in a lawsuit; this leads most people to say that animals do not have any legal rights. Second, we presently have the legal capacity, but not the political will, to protect all of the significant interests of animals, to enhance their welfare. In discussions within the animal-rights movement, those promoting welfare are considered a different group from those promoting legal rights. The gap between the two appears at first glance to be significant. Many individuals perceive that a call for animal rights is a call for equality of animals and humans and a significant threat to their meat-eating diet. But a careful look at where the legal system is today shows great complexity and a blurring of what many see as distinctly different worldviews.

(This material is discussed in law school under the heading of "standing." This is not a scholarly discussion of the topic but an introduction to some of the fundamental ideas. I do not seek to burden the reader with a string of Supreme Court opinions and legal jargon.)

It is not useful to focus on the question of whether an animal can file a lawsuit. That may be the highest level of acknowledgment for a rights holder, but it is not the threshold for being a rights holder. A better definition of a holder of legal rights is when at least one interest of an individual animal is acknowledged by some part of the legal system and the interest is taken into account by the courts or agencies separate from the human interests in making a decision. So, there are a series of preliminary questions that can be asked in order to reveal the complexity of the topic:

1. Does the entity in question (e.g., baby boy, New York City, your car, or your cat) have the capacity to hold a legal right? Does the entity possess personhood, or in this case animalhood?
2. Does the entity have protection from any legally recognized harm (e.g., freedom from physical beating by a human, or the need for food)?

3. May the entity file a lawsuit for its own protection from the legally recognized harm? May someone else seek protection for the entity from a legally recognized harm?

The problem of discussions to date is that if an individual answers point 3 in the negative, it is presumed that the answer to the first two questions is also negative. But a careful look at the status of animals within the law suggests otherwise.

Look at question 2: Are animal interests recognized within the law? The above discussion about wills, divorces, and trusts shows that the interests of animals in continuing to have the resources for a good life can be protected by the drafting of a trust for the benefit of named animals. So, in one small context, the interests of specific animals are acknowledged and protected by the law.

However, the most important and longstanding legal acknowledgment of animals can be found in the anticruelty laws of every state. In this short chapter I cannot set out all of the history of these laws, and I have done so elsewhere,[17] but here is the key point for our discussion today: The 1867 New York law pushed forward by Henry Berg made it a minor crime for the cruel beatings and needless killing of *any* animal.[18] As clarified by judges in subsequent court cases, the purpose of the law was to protect animals, not humans or the property interests of humans, but the animals themselves.

While the statutes of the fifty states today are not identical, the core principle is that humans should not be allowed to inflict unnecessary pain, suffering, or death upon an animal. This addresses both questions 1 and 2 above. The interests of animals are specifically acknowledged in the criminal laws of the states; in so doing, the legislature accepts that animals have legal personality. However, the law does not allow the animal itself to assert the protection provided by the law, as it is criminal matter; thus, the action in a specific fact pattern is filed by a representative of the state, usually a local prosecutor. Consequently, if Homer kicks Rover, Rover is unable to use the protections of the anticruelty statutes to file a case, but the local prosecutor could file a criminal complaint. (The state itself is the plaintiff in the case.) The prosecutor has full discretion to file or not file the case, which might best be characterized as a weak protection for Rover, but the concept is present and the possibly of punishment for violating Rover's rights exists.

However, while this analysis works well for companion animals, most states have a list of exceptions that usually include hunting and fishing and agricultural farm animals. These animals are within animal-human communities but without this legal right at present.

Might it be possible to do better for Rover? Yes. The state of North Carolina has adopted a law going one step further. The state has a typical anticruelty law plus one additional statute. The second law allows other humans or organizations to file a civil (not criminal) lawsuit for the enforcement of the criminal cruelty laws. So if Rover is in North Carolina, then his interests, his right to be free from unnecessary pain and suffering or his right to receive proper care, can be asserted in the courts by either a private party or the local prosecutor, or both.[19] Animalhood is more robust in North Carolina. There are only political reasons that stop the adoption of this law in all the states. Clearly Rover is intertwined in the legal system in ways that the ball cannot and should not be intertwined. There is no "ballhood."

Again, the interest of animals is acknowledged and will be taken into account by the court in making a ruling. Does this capacity of the court represent the animal's legal rights or welfare? I would claim it is both. Advocates for animal rights, however, reject this as welfare-ism and not rights law since it still remains that in North Carolina Rover may not put his name on the filing of the lawsuit as plaintiff. Rather than *Rover v. Smith*, he heading of the suit will be *Animal Defender v. Smith*, where Animal Defender is the lawyer for Rover. In North Carolina the evidence presented and the legal discussion before the judge will be about Rover (not Animal Defender's interests) whichever case heading is used. So, the reality is that Rover's interests are before the court and in my mind that is what constitutes the threshold of being a holder of legal rights.

Another example of a small step forward for the legal rights of animals is a 2016 Connecticut statute that allows attorneys or law students to be appointed to advocate for animals when a human is charged with a violation of the anticruelty law or when the owner has a hearing about custody of an animal. The statute states that an "advocate be appointed to represent the interests of justice."[20] This speaks in terms of justice rather than specifically allowing them to represent animals directly, as clients. But, clearly, the statute contemplates that such appointed individuals could present the court with information and suggestions about the best interests of the animal(s) at issue. It is just limited to dogs and cats. Goldfish have been left out, as well as birds, reptiles, rodents, and any other type animal one might keep as a pet. These are small, incremental steps forward into the arena of living property. Legal developments are showing increasing respect for some animals.

So some animals, in some areas of the law, have some legal rights. The animal-rights movement should accept the victory and move on to urge every state to adopt laws like those in North Carolina, Alaska, and Connecticut; find the resources to enhance enforcement of any existing legal rights; slowly expand the list of communities to which the rights apply; and expand the circumstance when their interests can be asserted (as in divorce proceedings).

Much more can be written about the nature of legal status, the nature and development of legal rights, and how the future of animal law might look. But that is for another book. This chapter is intended to support the idea that since animals are ethical subjects, they are presently limited legal persons with animalhood before the law. But their present status is inadequate to protect their interests. It is time to rethink the nature and extent of human obligations toward animals and to have the law reflect the respectful use of animals.

FINAL THOUGHTS

Thank you for reading this book. These chapters have taken you to many different places, so perhaps a summary of the major points will be helpful. The first issue addressed was whether or not animals should and could be part of the ethical world of each individual human. Since animals are living beings with interests of their own, they should appear in our ethical discussions as ethical subjects. But the more difficult question is, In what context should the consideration take place? The context is that of the specific community that we share with a particular animal. Additionally, the tool of analysis concerning a particular question is that of "respectful use." Choosing that path allows a more in-depth consideration of what the phrase "respectful use" contemplates.

Respect is a judgment, an output of the human brain. There are two primary paths for making judgement, the rational, verbal path and the holistic, rational but nonverbal path. Reflecting on how we make judgements had the advantage of allowing us to consider how other animals also make judgments. Understanding that at least mammals have roughly the same information-processing methods as we humans do, if not the same capacity for complexity, will, I hope, enhance our respect for these animals. Acknowledging that the human mind has two different methods of processing information is why fictional stories and poems are part of the book, helping the reader see issues from more than one perspective.

Accepting that animals are ethical subjects, the next critical question is, How much weight do their interests have when we are considering the consequences of our possible actions? While no numbers exist to measure this process, it is helpful to understand that the judgment will occur in the context of which shared community exists between a particular human and particular animal.

To provide the reader with some examples of how this might work, a number of issues, such as dogfighting or zoo animals, were considered, both in the context of individual ethical judgment and social ethical judgment that has been embedded in the law. Dogfighting is unethical, but keeping wildlife in zoos cannot call forth an easy answer. There are good zoos and bad zoos, so it depends. There are no good dogfights.

With some animals as ethical subjects, then the legal context of animals as property does not fit very well. What about our pets? If we accept them as ethical subjects, then we can think of them more readily as companions and us as their guardians. Many individuals have indeed moved at least companion animals out of the stodgy and constraining category of personal property. While portions of our law are breaking the property mold for some animal issues, there is a long way to go, and it will be better for them, and easier for us, if we think of them as a new category, that of living property.

Ultimately we are all riders on this spaceship Earth. Most of us believe that being alive is a good thing, which in turn should require us to admit that the lives of others are also good. And, therefore, we should do what we can to support other life while we support our own. At least some animals are "others" and both deserve and need our support. This can best be accomplished by showing respect and only making respectful use of animals. Indeed, as I suggest, we should all take upon ourselves a duty actively to support the lives of others, with our actions, our money, and our votes. It is relatively clear that governments and global corporations, which hold and control so much of the destructive power of humankind, do not have a priority of respect for others. If we, individual ethical actors, do not engage with each other and require the governments and global corporations to respect life, then in the time of just a few generations, life on Earth will be significantly diminished. The wave of life as we know it will lose strength and be at risk of breaking on the shoals. Enhance the Wave. What can you do?

Ripples and Waves

Rocks hit the Water.
My rock
And yours.
Will the Waves
Join,
Dissipate,
Negate,
Build into
The great Wave?

The future
is on the
Waves

Can we
Ride the
Waves?

Where will
We go?

Action

It's not about me,
It's about we,
We as in
Democracy.

POSTSCRIPT

The Future

Hope is a force,
Hope is a focus,
Hope is change.

What do you hope?

I hope for us,
I hope for you,
I hope the Wave
Rolls on.
Strong, vibrant, alive
Full of hope.

NOTES

The following references to books and many of the articles are for the reader who is interested in gaining more information about a topic. The references to websites might be either a source site or a citation of further information.

Foreword

1. This data comes from personal communications from veterinarian who tracks this information, 2005.

Introduction

1. For a consideration of this issue in a more scholarly analysis, see Robert Garner, *A Theory of Justice for Animals* (Oxford, NY: Oxford University Press, 2013); S. F. Sapontzis, *Morals, Reason, and Animals* (Philadelphia: Temple University Press, 1987).

2. See David Favre and Vivian Tsang, "The Development of Anti-Cruelty Laws during the 1800s," *Detroit College Law Review* 1 (1993), available online at: http://digitalcommons.law.msu.edu/facpubs/133/ (accessed January 19, 2018).

Chapter 1: An Ethical Duty Toward Animals

1. Statista, "Number of Dogs in the United States from 2000 to 2017 (in Millions)," https://www.statista.com/statistics/198100/dogs-in-the-united-states-since-2000/.

2. Steven Wise, *Drawing the Line* (Cambridge, MA: Perseus, 2002). The website for his organization has considerable legal materials about his battle for animal rights. Nonhuman Rights Project, 2018, https://www.nonhumanrights.org/ (accessed January 19, 2018).

3. Richard Dawkins, *The Selfish Gene* (Oxford and New York: Oxford University Press, paperback ed.1978), p. 65.

What is a single selfish gene trying to do? It is trying to get more numerous in the gene pool. Basically it does this by helping to program the bodies in which it finds itself to survive and to reproduce.

NOTES

Chapter 2: The Fork in the Road: The Use of Beings

1. See, generally, Gary Francione, *Animals, Property, and the Law* (Philadelphia: Temple University Press, 1995).

2. Gary Francione and Anna Charlton, "Animal Law: A Proposal for a New Direction," in Anne Peters, Saskia Stucki, and Livia Boscardin, eds., *Animal Law: Reform or Revolution* (Zurich and Basel: Schulthess, 2015).

3. Adapted from *Merriam-Webster*, s.v. "use (*v.*)," last modified December 19, 2017, https://www.merriam-webster.com/dictionary/use (accessed January 26, 2018).

Chapter 3: Respectful Use

1. From *Merriam-Webster*, s.v. "respect (*v.*)," last modified January 18, 2018, https://www.merriam-webster.com/dictionary/respect (accessed January 26, 2018).

2. Seymour Moskowitz, "Save the Children: The Legal Abandonment of American Youth in the Workplace," *Akron Law Review* 43, no. 107 (2010).

3. For example, under Michigan state law it is illegal to: (a) own, possess, use, buy, sell, offer to buy or sell, import, or export an animal for fighting or baiting, (b) be a party to or cause the fighting, baiting, or shooting of an animal, (c) rent a building, shed, room, yard, ground, or premises for fighting, baiting, or shooting an animal, (e) organize, promote, or collect money for the fighting, baiting, or shooting of an animal, (f) be present at a building, shed, room, yard, ground, or premises where preparations are being made for an exhibition, or be present at the exhibition, knowing that an exhibition is taking place or about to take place. Michigan Comp. Laws §750.49 (2).

4. This portion of the brain is known as Broca's area and is usually on the left side of the brain. Erin Harte, "Language Processing in the Human Brain," *Brain World*, September 29, 2017, http://brainworldmagazine.com/language-processing-in-the-human-brain/ (accessed January 26, 2018).

Chapter 4: The Property Status

1. David Favre and Peter Borchelt, *Animal Law and Dog Behavior* (Tucson: Lawyers & Judges Publishing, 1999), p. 25.

2. Gary Francione and Robert Garner, eds., *Animal Rights Debate* (New York: Columbia University Press, 2011), p. 1.

For the most part, when I refer to animal rights, I am really referring to one right: the right not to be treated as the property of humans.

Chapter 5: Introduction to Communities

1. "Principle of equal consideration" is discussed in Gary Francione, "Animals-Property or Persons," in *Animal Rights: Current Debates and New Directions*, ed. Cass Sunstein and Martha Nussbaum (Oxford and New York: Oxford University Press, 2004), p. 121.

2. See Jacob Bronowski, *Origins of Knowledge and Imagination* (New Haven and London: Yale University Press, 1978).

3. See generally Peter Singer, *Animal Liberation: A New Ethic for Our Treatment of Animals* (New York: Avon Press, 1975).

4. See Edward O. Wilson, *The Social Conquest of Earth* (New York: Liveright, 2013).

Chapter 6: Human Communities

1. Jeanne Batalova and Jie Zong, "Cuban Immigrants in the United States," Migration Policy Institute, November 9, 2017, https://www.migrationpolicy.org/article/cuban -immigrants-united-states (accessed January 19, 2018).

Chapter 7: Human Communities with Animals

1. See Doug Mellren, Associated Press, "Debate Continues after Death of Keiko," *Orlando Sentinel*, December 14, 2003; Keiko: The Untold Story of the Star of Free Willy, http://www .keikotheuntoldstory.com/about/keiko/thestory/ (accessed January 19, 2018).

2. I. Justinian, "On the Division of Things," *The Institutes of Justinian* (Book II, title 1 § 120), p. 66.

3. See Aldo Leopold, *Sand County Almanac* (Madison, WI: Tamarack, 1949; New York: Oxford University Press, 1977), pp. 201–26.

4. *Daily Commercial* (Leesburg, FL), December 15, 2003, pp. A2, A3.

5. See Krystof Obidzinski, "Fact File:—Indonesia World Leader in Palm Oil Production," Thomson Reuters Foundation News, July 9, 2013, http://www.trust.org/item/20130709022 623-zilwy/ (accessed January 19, 2018); Serge Wich et al., *The Future of the Bornean Orangutan: Impacts of Change in Land Cove* (Liverpool and Amsterdam: UNEP, 2015), http://issuu.com/ ungrasp/docs/unep_ou_eng_20150629.1.compressed (accessed January 19, 2018).

6. Humane Society of the United States, "Scientists and Experts on Battery Cages and Laying Hen Welfare," http://www.humanesociety.org/assets/pdfs/farm/HSUS-Synopsis-of -Expert-Opinions-on-Battery-Cages-and-Hen-Welfare.pdf (accessed January 19, 2018). For impactful images of confinement chickens, type "battery chickens" into Google Images.

7. See *Animal and Plant Health Inspection Service Report: "Annual Report Animal Usage by Fiscal Year"* (Washington, DC: United States Department of Agriculture, 2016), https:// www.aphis.usda.gov/animal_welfare/downloads/reports/Annual-Report-Animal-Usage -by-FY2016.pdf (accessed January 19, 2018).

8. See David Favre, *Animal Law: Welfare, Interests, and Rights*, 2nd ed. (New York: Wolter Kluwer, 2011), pp. 118–26.

9. Get our your checkbook and visit ViaGen Pets, https://viagenpets.com/ (accessed February 10, 2018).

10. GloFish, 2018, http://www.glofish.com/ (accessed January 19, 2018).

11. Antonio Regalado, "Human-Animal Chimeras Are Gestating on US Research Farms," *MIT Technology Review*, January 6, 2016, https://www.technologyreview.com/s/545106/human-animal-chimeras-are-gestating-on-us-research-farms/ (accessed January 19, 2018).

Chapter 8: We All Have Interests

1. Richard Dawkins, *The Selfish Gene* (Oxford and New York: Oxford Press, 1976).

2. Ibid., p. 21.

3. "It does not lie within the power of any judicial system to remedy all human wrongs. The obvious limitations upon the time of the courts, the difficulty in many cases of ascertaining the real facts or of providing any effective remedy, have meant that there must be some selection of those more serious injuries which have the prior claim to redress and are dealt with most easily. Trivialities must be left to other means of settlement, and many wrongs which in themselves are flagrant—ingratitude, avarice, broken faith, brutal words, and heartless disregard of the feelings of others—are beyond any effective legal remedy, and any practical administration of the law."

W. Page Keeton et al., *Prosser and Keeton on Torts*, 5th ed. (St. Paul, MN: West Publishing, 1984), p. 23.

4. Jocelyn Kaiser, "NIH Will Retire Most Research Chimps, End Many Projects," *Science*, June 26, 2013, http://www.sciencemag.org/news/2013/06/nih-will-retire-most-research-chimps-end-many-projects (accessed January 19, 2018).

Chapter 10: The Process of Making Judgments

1. See Michael S. Gazzaniga, *Who's in Charge? Free Will and the Science of the Brain* (New York: Ecco, an imprint of HarperCollins Publishers, 2011).

Chapter 11: Values

1. *Merriam-Webster*, s.v. "value (*n./v.*)," last modified January 26, 2018, https://www.merriam-webster.com/dictionary/value (accessed January 29, 2018).

2. See Thomas Friedman, *The Lexis and the Olive Tree, Understanding Globalization* (New York: Farrar, Straus, and Giroux, 1999).

3. Endangered Species Act of 1973, 16 U.S.C. §§ 1531–44.

4. Ibid., at §1539, which allows for the granting of permits under special conditions.

Chapter 12: Ethical Judgments about Animals

1. For two examples of roadside zoos not adequately caring for their animals, see: Animal Legal Defense Fund, "King Kong Zoo Permanently Shut Down after Being Sued by the Animal Legal Defense Fund," press release, February 23, 2017, http://aldf.org/press-room/press-releases/king-kong-zoo-permanently-shut-down-after-being-sued-by-the-animal-legal-defense-fund (accessed January 19, 2018). Animal Legal Defense Fund, "ALDF Calls Out Tennessee Animal House of Horror," press release, September 9, 2014, http://aldf.org/press-room/press-releases/aldf-calls-out-tennessee-animal-house-of-horror/ (accessed January 19, 2018).

2. Type "HSUS downer cows at slaughter house" into YouTube's search bar for access to videos about the horrible treatment of cows.

3. See Temple Grandin and Catherine Johnson, *Animals Make Us Human* (Boston & New York: Houghton Mifflin Harcourt, 2009), pp. 13–23.

4. See "Accreditation," Association of Zoos & Aquariums, September 2017, https://www.aza.org/accreditation/ (accessed January 19, 2018).

5. For background on the welfare issues of the world of dog racing and a list of states outlawing greyhound racing see: ""Fact Sheet: Greyhound Racing in the United States* (Arlington, MA: Grey2K USA Worldwide, 2016), https://www.grey2kusa.org/pdf/GREY2K_USA_National_Fact_Sheet.pdf (accessed January 19, 2018).

6. See Karyan Ng, "A Brief History of Fairtrade," Bean Market, May 2, 2016, https://beanmarket.com.au/brief-history-fairtrade/ (accessed February 20, 2018).

7. For more detail on the coffee free-trade topic, see Wikipedia, s.v. "Fair Trade Coffee," https://en.wikipedia.org/wiki/Fair_trade_coffee; International Coffee Organization, "History," http://www.ico.org/icohistory_e.asp?section=About_Us (accessed February 20,2018)

8. See "Shade Grown Coffee," Eartheasy, 2014, http://eartheasy.com/eat_shadegrown_coffee.htm (accessed January 19, 2018).

9. See Clarissa Wei, "The Myths of Medicinal Ivory," KCET, April 7, 2015, https://www.kcet.org/food/the-myths-of-medicinal-ivory (accessed January 19, 2018).

Chapter 13: We Are the Gods of Old

1. See Yue Wang, "More People Have Cell Phones than Toilets, UN Study Shows," *Time*, March 25, 2013, http://newsfeed.time.com/2013/03/25/more-people-have-cell-phones-than-toilets-u-n-study-shows/ (accessed January 19, 2018).

2. Ani Kame'enui, "Trump Infrastructure Proposal Could Devastate Public Lands," *National Parks Conservation Association*, February 16, 2018, https://www.npca.org/articles/1756-trump-infrastructure-proposal-could-devastate-public-lands (accessed February 20, 2018).

3. Elizabeth Pennisi," "Human Speech Gene Can Speed Learning in Mice," *Science*, September 15, 2014, http://www.sciencemag.org/news/2014/09/human-speech-gene-can

-speed-learning-mice (accessed January 19, 2018); Danielle Simmons, "The Use of Animal Models in Studying Genetic Disease: Transgenesis and Induced Mutation," *Nature Education* 1, no. 1 (2008): 70, https://www.nature.com/scitable/topicpage/the-use-of-animal-models-in -studying-855 (accessed January 19, 2018).

4. GloFish, https://shop.glofish.com/; for backstory see Wikipedia, s.v. "GloFish," https:// en.wikipedia.org/wiki/GloFish (accessed February 20, 2018).

5. Ian Sample, "First UK Baby with DNA from Three People Could Be Born Next Year," *Guardian*, December 15, 2016, https://www.theguardian.com/science/2016/dec/15/three -parent-embryos-regulator-gives-green-light-to-uk-clinics (accessed January 19, 2018). Also, California family law now specifically allows for a child to have more than two parents. CAL. FAM. CODE § 7601 (West 2014).

Chapter 14: Dealing with Death

1. Nebraska was an early state to outlaw the poisoning of animals, although limited to economically valuable animals such as horse and sheep. Neb. Stat. ch. 10 § 66 (1887). Most states today have a general prohibition against poisoning animals. Michigan makes the knowing administration of poison a felony with a possible four-year prison sentence. Mich. Comp. Laws. Anno. § 50b. (1).

2. In re Capers Estate, 34 Pa. D. & C.2nd 121 (1963), available at https://www.animallaw .info/case/re-capers-estate (accessed January 19, 2018).

3. For example, Montana allows the possession, but not the release of Pythons. MCA 87-5-706. See generally "Map of Private Exotic Pet Ownership Laws," Michigan State University, Animal Legal & Historical Center, 2017, https://www.animallaw.info/content/map-private -exotic-pet-ownership-laws (accessed January 19, 2018).

4. People v. Voelker, 658 N.Y.S.2nd 180 (1997).

5. "Thus, it is clear that the justification for killing or torturing the animals must be of the type necessary to preserve the safety of property or to overcome danger or injury." Ibid.

6. The animal suffering story is set out in many books, including: Gene Baur, *Farm Sanctuary* (New York & London: Touchstone, Simon & Schuster, 2008); *Putting Meat on the Table: Industrial Farm Animal Production in America* (Baltimore, MD: Pew Charitable Trusts at Johns Hopkins Bloomberg School of Public Health, 2008), http://www.pewtrusts.org/en/ research-and-analysis/reports/2008/04/29/putting-meat-on-the-table-industrial-farm-animal -production-in-america (accessed January 19, 2018).

7. Ruairí Arrieta-Kenna, "The Biggest Ever 'Dead Zone' in the Gulf of Mexico Is the Size of New Jersey," *Vox*, August 3, 2017, https://www.vox.com/science-and-health/2017/ 8/3/16089296/gulf-of-mexico-dead-zone (accessed January 19, 2018).

8. See Nicolette Hahn Niman, *Defending Beef: The Case for Sustainable Meat Production* (White River Junction, VT: Chelsea Green Publishing, 2014).

9. See Joel Salatin, *Everything I Want to Do Is Illegal* (Swoope, VA: Polyface; White River

Junction, VT: Chelsea Green, 2007). For a full list of his books explaining and promoting the pasture raising of animals, see "Joel Salatin," Amazon, 2018, https://www.amazon.com/Joel -Salatin/e/B000APFOT2/ref=ntt_dp_epwbk_0 (accessed January 19, 2018).

10. See Michael Pollan, *Omnivore's Dilemma* (New York: Penguin, 2006).

11. See the Fence Row Farm You Tube channel: "2013 08 07 15 27 03," YouTube video, 0:25, Icelandic sheep in the shade on a hot day, posted by "Fence Row Farm," February 16, 2015, https://www.youtube.com/watch?v=wo9Q4kMGVOA (accessed January 19, 2018).

12. Jocelyn Kaiser, "NIH Will Retire Most Research Chimps, End Many Projects," *Science*, June 26, 2013, http://www.sciencemag.org/news/2013/06/nih-will-retire-most-research -chimps-end-many-projects (accessed January 19, 2018).

13. The federal Animal Welfare acts directs the adoption of regulations in part as follows:

> (2)(A) for handling, housing, feeding, watering, sanitation, ventilation, shelter from extremes of weather and temperatures, adequate veterinary care, and separation by species where the Secretary finds necessary for humane handling, care, or treatment of animals; and
> (3) with respect to animals in research facilities, include requirements—
> (A) for animal care, treatment, and practices in experimental procedures to ensure that animal pain and distress are minimized, including adequate veterinary care with the appropriate use of anesthetic, analgesic, tranquilizing drugs, or euthanasia;
> (B) that the principal investigator considers alternatives to any procedure likely to produce pain to or distress in an experimental animal;
> 7 USC §§ 2142. Absence from the law is any focus upon which experiments are undertaken.

14. "Ban on Animal Testing," European Commission, last updated January 30, 2018, https://ec.europa.eu/growth/sectors/cosmetics/animal-testing_en (accessed January 30, 2018).

Chapter 15: Do Ethics Operate within or upon Global Corporations and Governments?

1. One of the most extraordinary, insightful examinations of the seeking and use of political power is the story of Lyndon Johnson's rise to the presidency of the United States from the back country of Texas, as examined by Robert Caro. For a quick summary of the four-volume series and the impact of the books, see Wikipedia, s.v. *"The Years of Lyndon Johnson,"* last edited January 10, 2018, https://en.wikipedia.org/wiki/The_Years_of_Lyndon_Johnson (accessed January 19, 2018).

2. Anthony Barbera and Virginia McConnell, "Effects of Pollution Control on Industry Productivity," *Journal of Industrial Economics* 35, no. 161 (1986).

Also, in 1972, the industry made a major process change, from the sulfite process for pulping to the draft process, as a result of environmental regulations designed to control sulfur dioxide (p. 169).

Also see Allan Springer, *Industrial Environmental Control: Pulp and Paper Industry* (New York & Chichester: John Wiley & Sons, 1986), pp. 3–4.

3. See background information from, "Farm Animal Welfare: Chickens," Massachusetts Society for the Protection and Care of Animals, 2018, https://www.mspca.org/animal_protection/farm-animal-welfare-chickens/ (accessed January 19, 2018).

4. Associated Press, "China's Lenovo Acquires IBM Division," NBC News, May 1, 2005, http://www.nbcnews.com/id/7695811/ns/business-world_business/t/chinas-lenovo-acquires-ibm-division/#.WmI9S66nGM8 (accessed January 19, 2018).

5. For full details of the process, see Jason Zhang, "Summary and Analysis of Mergers between Global Seed Companies in 2016," *Agro News*, March 1, 2017, http://news.agropages.com/News/NewsDetail---21186.htm (accessed January 19, 2018). Then, in 2017, more merger talks were underway, "Bayer, Monsanto Start $2.5 Billion Asset Sale to Get Merger Clearance," Reuters, March 9, 2017, http://www.reuters.com/article/us-monsanto-m-a-bayer-idUSKBN16G1PB (accessed January 19, 2018).

6. Danny Hakim, "Auto Supplier Delphi Files for Bankruptcy," *New York Times*, October 9, 2005, http://www.nytimes.com/2005/10/09/business/auto-supplier-delphi-files-for-bankruptcy.html (accessed January 19, 2018).

7. See Ballotpedia, "California Proposition 2, Standards for Confining Farm Animals (2008)," https://ballotpedia.org/California_Proposition_2,_Standards_for_Confining_Farm_Animals_(2008) (accessed Feb 2018).

8. "Walmart US Announces New Animal Welfare and Antibiotics Positions," Walmart, May 22, 2015, https://corporate.walmart.com/_news_/news-archive/2015/05/22/walmart-us-announces-new-animal-welfare-and-antibiotics-positions (accessed January 19, 2018). In 2017, McDonald's announced a more robust commitment to animal welfare. McDonald's, "McDonald's Announces Commitments to Advancements in Chicken Welfare," press release, October 27, 2017, http://news.mcdonalds.com/Corporate/news-stories/2017/McDonald-s-Announces-Commitments-to-Advancements-i (accessed January 19, 2018).

9. Steve Boggan, "'We Blew It': Nike Admits to Mistakes Over Child Labor," *Independent/ UK*, October 20, 2001, https://www.commondreams.org/headlines01/1020-01.htm (accessed January 19, 2018). Also see Matt Wilsey and Scott Lichtig, "The Nike Controversy," (essay; Stanford, CA: Stanford University), https://web.stanford.edu/class/e297c/trade_environment/wheeling/hnike.html (accessed January 19, 2018).

Chapter 16: A Foray into the Law

1. For a course book on animal law, see David Favre, *Animal Law: Welfare, Interests, and Rights*, 2nd ed. (New York: Wolters Kluwer, 2011).

2. Beginning in 2013, the Nonhuman Rights Project has sought to have the courts of New York allow habeas corpus petition lawsuits in the name of several chimpanzees. See Nonhuman Rights Project, 2018, http://www.nonhumanrightsproject.org/ (accessed January 30, 2018), and the case report at 2015 WL 4612340. In June of 2017, a New York appeals court rejected the claims on behalf of the chimpanzees (2017 NY Slip Opinion 04574).

3. Dred Scott v. Sandford, 60 U.S. 393 (1856). All nine judges wrote opinions, but the vote was six to two against Mr. Scott. He was found not to be a citizen of the US and therefore without legal personhood, or rather, without the capacity to sue.

4. See David Favre and Vivian Tsang, "The Development of Anti-Cruelty Laws During the 1800's," *Detroit College Law Review* 1 (1993), available at http://digitalcommons.law.msu.edu/facpubs/133/ (accessed January 19, 2018).

5. David Favre, "Living Property: A New Status for Animals within the Legal System," *Marquette Law Review* 93, no. 1021 (2010), available at: http://digitalcommons.law.msu.edu/facpubs/136/ (accessed January 19, 2018).

6. The Uniform Probate Code on wills was implemented in Arizona law in 1994 and is still effective today. (See, e.g., Ariz. Rev. Stat. Ann. § 14–2907, "(B) A trust for the care of a designated domestic or pet animal is valid.")

7. See Cara Buckley, "Cosseted Life and Secret End of a Millionaire Maltes," *New York Times*, June 9, 2011, http://www.nytimes.com/2011/06/10/nyregion/leona-helmsleys-millionaire-dog-trouble-is-dead.html (accessed January 19, 2018).

8. Amy B. Wang, "A Divorcing Couple Asked a Judge to Treat Their Dogs like Children. Here Is His Reply," *Washington Post*, December 21, 2016, http://wpo.st/RsrO2 (accessed January 19, 2018).

9. David Grimm, *Citizen Canine* (New York: Public Affairs, 2014); also see Alvin Chang, "When My Dog Died, I Didn't Understand Why It Felt like a Human had Died. Then I Read the Research," *Vox*, July 11, 2016, http://www.vox.com/2016/7/11/12109786/dog-death-research (accessed January 19, 2018); Lois Smith Brady, "If Anyone Here Objects to This Union, Bark," *New York Times*, April 29, 2016, https://www.nytimes.com/2016/05/01/fashion/weddings/dogs-cats-and-other-pets-at-weddings.html (accessed January 19, 2018).

10. Karin Brulliard, "In a First, Alaska Divorce Courts Will Now Treat Pets More like Children," *Washington Post*, January 24, 2017, https://www.washingtonpost.com/news/animalia/wp/2017/01/24/in-a-first-alaska-divorce-courts-will-now-treat-pets-more-like-children/?utm_term=.773b4e4024cb (accessed January 19, 2018).

11. Alaska Stat. §25.24.160(a).

12. Leonor Vivanco-Prengaman, "New State Law Treats Pets More like Children in Custody Cases," *Chicago Tribune*, December 25, 2017, http://www.chicagotribune.com/news/local/breaking/ct-met-pet-custody-law-20171218-story.html (accessed January 19, 2018).

13. For a detailed consideration of this issue, see David Favre, "Equitable Self-Ownership for Animals," *Duke Law Journal* 50, no. 473 (2000), available at: http://digitalcommons.law.msu.edu/facpubs/190/ (accessed January 19, 2018).

NOTES

14. Michigan Department of Natural Resources, Wildlife Division, "Michigan Black Bear Digest," May 1–June 1, 2017, https://www.michigan.gov/documents/dnr/Bear_Hunting _Digest_454168_7.pdf (assessed February 24, 2018).

15. For a detailed consideration of this issue, see David Favre, "Wildlife Rights," *University of Oregon Journal of Environmental Law and Litigation* 25, no. 459 (2010), available at: http:// digitalcommons.law.msu.edu/facpubs/194/ (accessed January 19, 2018).

16. In an interview with the hunter:

> **Bakst:** You've expressed some regret over the way this transpired. Is your regret about taking this lion or being kind of caught up in this whole swirl?
>
> **Palmer:** I made an initial statement on that and I'm going to stay true to that, OK? Obviously, if I'd have known this lion had a name and was that important to the country, or a study, obviously, I wouldn't have taken it.

"Full Transcript: Walter Palmer Speaks about Cecil the Lion Controversy," *StarTribune*, September 7, 2015, http://www.startribune.com/full-transcript-walter-palmer-speaks-about -controversy/325453351/ (accessed February 26, 2018). For more details of the story, see Wikipedia, s.v. "Killing of Cecil the Lion," last edited January 29, 2018, https://en.wikipedia .org/wiki/Killing_of_Cecil_the_lion (accessed January 30, 2018).

17. Favre and Tsang, "Development of Anti-Cruelty Laws."

18. Ibid.

19. North Carolina Gen. Statutes Anno. § 19A-2. ("It shall be the purpose of this Article to provide a civil remedy for the protection and humane treatment of animals in addition to any criminal remedies that are available.") This law is discussed in detail in a law review article, William Reppy Jr., "Citizen Standing to Enforce Anti-Cruelty Laws by Obtaining Injunctions: The North Carolina Experience," *Animal Law* 11, no. 39 (2005).

20. Conn. Gen. Statute Anno. § 54–86n. See Laurel Wamsley, "In a First, Connecticut's Animals Get Advocates in the Courtroom," NPR, June 2, 2017, http://www.npr.org/sections/ thetwo-way/2017/06/02/531283235/in-a-first-connecticuts-animals-get-advocates-in-the -courtroom (accessed January 19, 2018).

INDEX

INDEX

INDEX

INDEX

INDEX